THE *Almost* EMPTY NESTER

Rediscover Who You Are
BEFORE Your Kids Leave the Nest

KARLA OLSON

SB
PRESS

Published by StoryBuilders Press

Hardcover: 978-1-954521-55-1
Paperback: 978-1-954521-54-4
eBook: 978-1-954521-56-8
Audio: 978-1-954521-53-7

THANK YOU TO MY READERS

Now that I have two daughters out of the house and one about to graduate, I am hyper aware of the impact I had on my mother when I left our home thirty-six years ago. When my first daughter went off to college in 2019, I began to truly understand what my mom felt like when I left. That empty space in her heart where I had once occupied daily, her changing identity, and the depth of her emotions were now happening to me.

I was feeling the heartache that comes with your first child moving out and getting a good glimpse of what life would be like in the near future. I knew this Empty Nest chapter was going to be a challenge if I didn't face it head-on. I needed to start preparing. I wanted to dream about what my future could look like in a few years and intentionally create one of the best chapters of my life.

I want the same for you.

From the moment I started writing this, I hoped that the right reader would find it and benefit from all the teachings inside. We are about to take an amazing journey together, and I can't wait to see the positive impact it has on your life!

If you haven't already, join our community at
theemptynesterclub.com

CONTENTS

A NOTE TO MY DAUGHTERS

As you're getting ready to leave the nest and go on your merry way
I want to pause and take a minute to share a few things I need to say.

This time in our life is filled with new and exciting changes for you and me.
It's been my joy to watch you grow up and be exactly who you're meant to be.

As I watch you pack your bags and make exciting new plans for yourself,
Don't mind me when I start to pull those old scrapbooks off the shelf.

They say your children only stay little for a very short moment in time.
They grow into young adults in what feels like the blink of an eye.

I couldn't be prouder of who you are and the person you've become.
It brings happy tears to my eyes and makes my joyful heart hum.

I want to thank the younger you for moments that will never be replaced.
Especially the thousands of sweet little kisses you left upon my face.

I hope you have the time of your life. Go out into the world and shine bright.
Always remember, I'm just a phone call away, and never dim your bright light.

Love, Mom

FOREWORD

Thanks to technology our world has evolved so that almost anything can now be solved with a "quick fix." All hail Amazon Prime and next-day delivery. Out of sunscreen? Click "buy now" and have it on your front door the next day. Forgot the dress you need for the beach trip? Rush ship it, and you're ready to go.

As mothers, our lives have revolved for years around managing, fixing, cultivating, and pressing that quick-ship button for our children. And then, if we've done our job well, our children exit our well-managed, well-oiled nest and head out to the next stage of their lives. We post pictures of their progress, successes, and achievements, proud as peacocks. But what about us? What happens behind the scenes in that now-empty nest?

There's good news and tough news. The unavoidable truth is that there is no quick-fix or buy-now button to fill that now-empty nest, and, in today's society, that's a hard pill to swallow. That's the tough news. The good news? Finally, we have an author who has taken a deep, introspective look at Empty Nesting and laid out a comprehensive roadmap for us based on thoughtful preparation to tackle this important topic.

In 1980, a young girl wearing a parochial red and gray plaid school uniform walked into my life and forever changed it. I have been lucky enough to weather the deep storms of grade school, high school, and college with Karla Olson and, perhaps most importantly, the birth and raising of our children. Years later, we have supported each other through another incredibly important phase; the seismic shift within our lives as we have launched our children from our respective homes out into the world.

Watching Karla tackle this enormous challenge facing mothers has been awe-inspiring. What started as an idea turned into a passion project and then a well-formed, data-backed plan to support women as they journey into the unknowns of Empty Nesting. Karla is like a force of nature once she gets started and has left no stone unturned with her desire to help women truly prepare for this enormous life shift.

I have been fortunate to have Karla by my side throughout many of life's more challenging moments. I know firsthand her skill sets of motivation, data-gathering, and her deep desire to empower women. It brings me great joy to know that through her new book, her readers will learn what a gift she is to the world.

The Almost Empty Nester will welcome you to take an introspective look at the amazing journey you have traveled so far and offer you a roadmap of preparation for your next, best chapter. This book is not just a guide; it's a companion, a source of comfort, and a beacon of hope for those of us standing at the threshold of a new beginning. Karla's insights and strategies are a lifeline, providing clarity and confidence as we navigate this transition. So, take a deep breath, embrace the change, and get ready to rediscover yourself in this next exciting phase of life.

Cristina Horvath
Sweet Pea Ink Creative

INTRODUCTION

My grandparents purchased tickets for the maiden voyage of the *Titanic* a few weeks before it was scheduled to leave for New York. Their luggage was carefully loaded onto the ship, including my grandfather's two suitcases and everything my grandmother owned. She was young, newly married, and brimming with excitement to see America for the very first time.

However, a few days before *Titanic*'s departure, they made a crucial decision. My grandfather had been receiving urgent telegrams from his New York–based company pleading with him to come home early. And so they did. With a little luck, they bought two last-minute tickets on the sister ship, the *Olympic*, and set sail for New York. They quickly boarded with only two small carry-ons and made it to America days before *Titanic* tragically sank at sea. They lost almost everything they owned, but because of that one decision, my dad became a possibility.

Fast-forward to 1930. My mom's future parents were friends, but at the time, were engaged to other people. After a while, they both realized they were madly in love with each other, so they summoned up the courage to break off their engagements. Because they followed their hearts and made the choice to marry soon after, my mom became a possibility.

And when my mom in her early twenties flew alone to Japan, met my dad, and married him on the spot, I became a possibility against all odds. I feel so lucky to be alive, and I'm incredibly grateful for my parents. What are the chances that I am here? That my kids are here? I can't help but feel like life is just one big miracle.

As my children have grown up and started moving out, I've spent the last several years reminiscing and reflecting on my own journey as a mother. The privilege, joy, and sacredness of it all. I am struck with awe by the sheer miracle of life itself, and that deepens as I watch my adult children venture out into the world, making their own choices, writing their own history. I find myself wondering where the time went from the breathtaking arrival of my babies to the young, independent adults they have grown into today. How precious time is and how fast it flies by continues to astonish me, especially as I grow older.

Empty Nesting redefines a mother's life in an instant and causes massive change. This transition sparks intense feelings we, as mothers, don't openly talk about or really understand how to prepare for. It's a monumental occasion we are often left to deal with alone, and it's one of the most impactful seasons of our lives. Most of us spent years going to school preparing for our first career, years dating before we found a life partner, and years raising our children. So why don't we apply this same rigor when preparing for Empty Nesting? "Who am I without my kids?" becomes the all-too-common question middle-aged moms are desperately trying to answer. We are so happy for and proud of our children when they grow up, graduate, and move out. But simultaneously, and often in silence, we mourn their leaving and our own changing identity. There's an unspoken societal expectation tied to Empty Nesting: "This isn't about you." "Be happy for them." "Don't be selfish." "Don't ruin their moment."

Except . . . it *is* about us, and it *is* our moment too, in a way that's different from what society narrates, projects, and portrays.

It's a rite of passage for both our children and us as mothers, and it's significant. Sometimes it's wonderful and exciting, but oftentimes it can be difficult and lonely. It's a defining moment for us all, and as Kevin Costner so eloquently says in the movie *Tin Cup*, "You either define the moment, or the moment defines you."[1] We need to learn how to prepare for this change so we can successfully navigate these unchartered waters, alongside being excited for and proud of our beautiful birdies leaving the nest.

This book is a landing place for everyone who has gone through or is about to go through this major life transition. Yes, others have sailed before us, but history has shown that most of us don't have a plan. According to the 2020 census, there's a whopping 22.5 million Empty Nesters in the United States alone.[2] From my experience coaching Empty Nesters, very few moms are prepared for when this happens. We need to start planning for Empty Nesting long before our kids graduate high school. If we start this process earlier, we won't be so emotionally blindsided the day they move out.

"You either define the moment, or the moment defines you."

When your child starts driving, for example, they become a little more independent from you. It's new to them, and it's new to you. It's a perfect time for growth and expansion, not just for them, but for you as well. By starting to see yourself as a separate individual again, not solely through the lens of motherhood, you will be more prepared and excited for what's to come.

I love being a mother and everything that comes with it. Well, almost everything. Let's keep it real. There's so much gratitude I have for the meals we've shared at our family table, the incredible trips we've taken together, and the laughter and life lessons we've experienced along the way. However, when our kids started moving out, my daily rhythm changed . . . a lot. After parenting for nearly two decades, I felt like I was finally coming up for air, engrossed with the unshakable desire for self-rediscovery. Can you relate? If so, you're in the right place.

When's the last time you thought to yourself, "What do *I* need? What do *I* want to do when my kids leave the house? What fulfills *me*? What are *my* gifts? What's *my* inner voice telling me, and why have I silenced her?" (And when did we learn to do that?!) Many of us are struggling to answer these universal questions. I want every talented, amazing mother and soon-to-be Empty Nester to fall in love with her future.

> *I want every talented, amazing mother and soon to be Empty Nester to fall in love with her future.*

This book is a compass that shows you how to find your way back to your previous passions and direct you forward into a brand-new future that YOU are going to start creating now! It's your map back to yourself. I have divided this book into the following three sections to help you discover what's possible for you in this next phase of your life:

 THE PAST: Take a moment to pause and reflect on what you've created. (It's amazing, and it's a lot.)

 THE PRESENT: Evaluate and honor where you are today. (This is a good time to take inventory and rediscover your interests.)

 THE FUTURE: Define what you want for your Empty Nesting years. (Take time to dream, create a plan, and design how you're going to do it.)

The stories and lessons inside will help you uncover your hopes and dreams as you begin to create your game plan for your best Empty Nest. You will gain clarity, insight, and awareness as you navigate this book. It's crucial to do this work before you move forward, and it will make the road ahead much more fun and a bit less bumpy. Together, let's design one of the most fulfilling chapters of your life. And by the way, if someone hasn't told you in a while, you're an incredible mom. I think you're amazing, and I'm so glad you are here.

xoxo,

Kayla

SECTION I

Past

CHAPTER 1

Hello, Stranger!
Where Have You Been?

Coming home to yourself is the most important journey you'll ever take. It's where you'll find your heart, your courage, your voice, your compass, your joy, your authenticity.

—JENNIFER LOUDEN

It was a beautiful sunny day on May 31, 2019, when my first daughter graduated from high school. As the ceremony came to a close, everyone gathered on the field to congratulate their brand-new graduates and take tons of priceless pictures. Through the smiles and tears, parents were talking about how they couldn't believe their babies had just graduated and how fast time had gone by. One conversation I heard over and over that day really stuck with me. Parents were repeatedly exclaiming to each other, "Wow! You're almost an Empty Nester, what are you going to do? I'm so not ready for that!"

That question instantly stopped me in my tracks.

I thought to myself, "I'm so glad I don't have to answer that today." At the time, I hadn't given much thought to Empty Nesting because I still had six years until my youngest child would be flying our nest. However, for many parents, it was their youngest graduating and moving out, and they were discussing through the tears how best to handle this life-changing milestone. They were about to become Empty Nesters for the first time, and their energy was different. You could feel the enormous pride and happiness they had for their high school graduates, but they seemed to carry a heavier weight on their shoulders than the other parents. Most of them couldn't answer the "What's next for you?" question as they sat with the gravity of change that was about to take place.

As summer rolled on, I witnessed these parents enjoying as much quality time as they could before their teens departed for college, the military, or first jobs. They took vacations, swam at the beach, had cookouts, shopped for dorm room supplies, and like any good, neurotic parent of a recent graduate does, squeezed in as much last-minute advice as they could. Everything seemed fine on the surface, and summer breezed by. But when move-out day was fast approaching, they resembled nothing of the carefree parents they had been all summer. Instead, they looked disoriented, depressed, and even a bit confused. Confused as in, "Now what will I do with my time?"

That fall, when we experienced our first college drop-off, so much of our family's daily life changed in an instant. Our dinner table grew smaller, younger siblings had to adjust, and the house got a little quieter. We really missed her sense of humor and laughter. She is so witty and wise. During our last family dinners leading up to the drop-off, I found myself staring across the table at my oldest envisioning the younger version of her in pigtails, just like Steve Martin did in the movie *Father of the Bride*. I kept thinking, "How is she already going off to college in September? Where did the time go? And how did she grow up so fast?"

If you are going through this, or are about to go through this, I'm not going to lie, it was tough. There's so much to process. I was beaming with excitement for her, remembering my own journey of leaving the nest and the fun that awaited, but I also felt this deep ache in my heart. It was a tricky time for me because I still had two daughters at home who needed me to be present for them. I was a very busy happy mom, so I got used to the change and discomfort as best I could, focused on the positive, and soldiered on.

Fast-forward to fall of 2022 when my second daughter left for college. Those three years went by so quickly, and I still couldn't answer those daunting questions "Who am I without my children around all the time?" and "What am I going to do when I become an Empty Nester?" I knew the next three years with my youngest daughter were going to fly by even faster. It became impossible to ignore the fact that I still had no idea what I wanted to do now that my children were all grown-up.

However, I did know this one thing: I wanted to learn how to prepare for Empty Nesting proactively and intentionally. To get excited about it while simultaneously missing my girls. I did not want to roll into this next phase a total hot mess! I wanted to fall in love with my future again, and I bet you do too.

For over two years, I have immersed myself in research and am blown away by the data I compiled about Empty Nesting. What started out as a passion project to help myself through this process has turned into my Empty Nest purpose: to help millions of women thrive in this season, rise to their highest calling, and define their midlife milestones (past), meaning (present), and mission (future). Why? When one woman rises, we all rise. I believe we all deserve to experience Empty Nesting as one of the most rewarding chapters of our lives.

WE NEED TO TALK

Often parents don't acknowledge that Empty Nesting is fast approaching until their last child moves out. It's human nature to delay and procrastinate preparing for the inevitable, just like registering your child for summer camp or packing for vacation. However, when new Empty Nesters walk into their profoundly silent home for the first time, it can hit them hard, realizing they're unprepared and ill equipped for this season. Heck, my house is already quieter than it's ever been as my youngest finishes up her senior year of high school. She's gone ten hours a day!

I am an "Almost Empty Nester," living through exactly what I am writing about. Even though big changes are coming, I'm committed to enjoying this last year with my youngest while simultaneously designing my next chapter. By taking myself through this book and the exercises within, I am more prepared this time around for the familiar loss I know I will feel. However, now I am filled with hope and excitement for her future and mine as well. My wish is for this book to find its way to every mother who wants more fulfillment and joy in their Empty Nesting years.

When one woman rises, we all rise.

When I researched the topic about preparing the mother for her Empty Nest, I found very limited resources. It was then I felt the need to create a powerful process to help women reclaim their unique identity and design their next best chapter. There were several incredible books written on Empty Nesting covering important topics such as navigating college orientations, saying goodbye, and building a stronger marriage. But there wasn't a single book or program addressing how to help the mother individually prepare her soul for this massive transition.

I was shocked when I discovered the lack of resources around this topic and knew that a book needed to be written specifically for mothers. They deserve a trusted adviser to guide them through this journey and help them develop a game plan for this phase of life. That is when I began my two and a half years of research, wrote this book, developed my transformational course, and created an online community for Empty Nest women.

I feel incredibly lucky to be a mom to three daughters. It is one of the most important and beloved roles of my life. However, throughout the jam-packed years of being a mom, I lost touch with myself a little bit along the way, and maybe you have too. That's okay. It's normal. You are not alone. Mothers frequently put their own hopes and dreams on the back burner for the sake of others. My good friend and author, Brittany Anderson, calls this the juggle struggle. It's the undeniable reality that as mothers, we often find ourselves trying to balance the myriad of responsibilities that come with raising children, managing a household, and maintaining a career. This relentless balancing act can lead to feelings of overwhelm and exhaustion, as the quest to meet everyone's needs seems never ending. However, when we take a moment to turn into the values that guide our decision-making and gain clarity on what truly matters, the fog of overwhelm and the loss of our sense of self begins to lift. Priorities become clearer, and we can now hear our soul whispers again.

It's time to tune some of that incredible loving energy back into ourselves. I've always had these little soul whispers of things that I've wanted to do, and I bet you have them too. Soul whispers are those internal nudges from your deepest wishes, dreams, and desires that you may have been ignoring for some time now. Let's bring them back into the light, craft a vision, and weave them into your beautiful story.

When it comes to Empty Nesting, there are a few key touch points needing to take place long before college drop-off or move-out day happens. This book fills in those gaps by offering a framework filled with tips, tools, and reflection exercises to help you get back in touch with yourself months, or even years, before your kids leave the nest. By doing this work, you will be better equipped and prepared for that pivotal moment.

Hands down, the world needs your gifts. Like yesterday.

As you prepare to enter this phase of life, take a moment and ask yourself, "What desires and wishes have I been holding back or suppressing?" "What do I love to do?" "What am I naturally good at?" "What talent or story of mine could I share with the world to make it a better place?" Hands down, the world needs your gifts. Like yesterday.

After my second daughter went off to college, I realized I had been playing small, neglecting my own aspirations and dreams while prioritizing the needs of everyone else. I began to fade into the background of my own life, all while projecting an image of unwavering strength and support to those around me. This was not something I wanted my daughters to witness anymore, so I committed to changing myself and my choices, immediately.

They now see their mom expressing herself more, taking up space, and following her own dreams while simultaneously encouraging others to follow theirs. Not honoring my individual desires for years was like trying to hold a beach ball underwater. It was exhausting and wasn't benefitting anyone, especially my family. Can you relate? Do you do this too? I knew at this point in my life, I needed to muster up some courage and let my dreams rise to the surface again. I needed to make a plan, take action, and do the work.

SELF-CARE IS NOT SELFISH

When I look back at why I had suppressed some of my own dreams over the years, I discovered I had a false belief around self-care and self-development. I was afraid if I did something for myself, it meant I wasn't focused on my family. Do you have this belief too? And if so, for how long? This belief couldn't be farther from the truth, and it's a common lie many of us tell ourselves. The sooner you focus some energy back onto yourself, the better you can serve your family. It benefits everyone when a mother's soul is deeply fulfilled and sets such an important example for your children to fill up their own cup and follow their dreams with gusto.

When you get through this book and finish the accompanying Reflection Exercises, you will have newfound clarity and inspiration about what you want for your Empty Nesting years. Imagine the effect you could have on your children after they see you go through this transformation. They just might say to you, "Wow, Mom, look at everything you have planned to do! It's amazing. You are such an inspiration to me. I'm so proud of you." Wouldn't that be a great way to prepare for your Empty Nest? I know that's what I want!

Here is a beautiful quote from Marianne Williamson that someone once sent to me as a reminder that everyone deserves to shine:

> Our deepest fear is not that we are inadequate. Our deepest fear is that we are powerful beyond measure. It is our light, not our darkness that most frightens us. We ask ourselves, "Who am I to be brilliant, gorgeous, talented, fabulous?" Actually, who are you not to be? Your playing small does not serve the world . . . There is nothing enlightened about shrinking so that other people won't feel insecure around you. We are all meant to shine.[3]

The Almost Empty Nester is more than just a book. It's an invitation to help you reflect on your past, assess where you are today, design what you want to create for your future, and most importantly, show you how to get there. And when you finish this book, you will have a beautiful, unique game plan for your next best chapter. We are going to design the Empty Nest of your dreams!

AS WE MOVE FORWARD

When your children start to move out, it's hard. But I've got a map: the compass back to your soul whispers. I am here to cheer you on as you prepare for your own Empty Nest. We are about to go through an amazing process together.

My personal mission is to uplift and impact one million Empty Nesters to rediscover their passion and purpose with clarity, courage, connection, and community, and it starts with you. I can't wait to help mothers successfully navigate what I just went through.

At the end of each chapter, you will have the opportunity to process what you just read and apply the teachings to your personal experiences. Take time to reflect and answer the questions before you move on to the next chapter. In the end, you will be glad you did! The more you put in, the more you will get out. There's science behind each concept and the order in which I present them, so aim to complete each Reflection Exercise before moving on to the next chapter. Each one is important for your growth and journey and key to your transformation.

It's time to grab your favorite journal, get yourself something yummy to drink, and sink down into a cozy spot so you can get to work on these concepts.

Life is not a dress rehearsal, and your Empty Nesting years will come faster than you think. I encourage you to start preparing for them now. The world needs your light and each one of your gifts. I'm so excited for you and can't wait to help you on your journey. Let's get to the good stuff.

It's time for your first reflection exercise! Let's observe where you are right now before we dive deeper into the past in Chapter 2.

Whether you're an Almost Empty Nester or brand-new Empty Nester, I'm glad you have found this book. I encourage you to share it with any friends who need it and join our community at theemptynesterclub.com.

Welcome to the club!

Chapter 1 Reflection Exercise

I invite you to take a moment and reflect on the questions below. It's important to take inventory of where you are at right now in your life so you can build upon your answers as you move through each exercise in the book. Ask yourself these questions:

- What are my thoughts and beliefs about Empty Nesting?

- How have I shown up for myself alongside being a present and engaged mom?

- What are some personal dreams I set aside over the years for the sake of others?

- What are some new skills I want to learn at this stage of my life?

- What makes me excited to get up in the morning?

- What activities light me up from within and make me lose track of time?

- What do I want to experience in this next phase of my life?

If you're having trouble conjuring up previous dreams or deciding what to do in the next phase of your life, let me reassure you that is completely normal. Give yourself some grace. Instead, take five minutes to brainstorm a list of anything and everything you might want to do if you had no time constraints. You can narrow it down as you move forward in the process. For now, just give yourself the chance to consider all the possibilities!

As you close your journal and set down your pen, remember that reflecting on and answering each of these questions honestly is an important first step toward creating your Empty Nest dream. And when you get to the end of the book, it will be fun to go back and reflect on the growth you've gone through during this creative process.

Next, let's talk a little bit about Empty Nest Syndrome and how you can choose thriving over just surviving during this next season.

What to Expect during Empty Nesting

Learning to Thrive

*Give the ones you love wings to fly, roots
to come back, and reasons to stay.*

—THE DALAI LAMA

I f you have kids in junior high and high school, it's never too early to begin thinking about Empty Nesting. When your children leave the nest, it's one of the biggest transitions in life. It's an exciting time, but if you aren't prepared, it can quickly become overwhelming and lonely. There are millions of Empty Nesters worldwide facing difficult emotions every day, and they deserve to have tools to not only help them get through it but thrive in it.

When I began to research Empty Nesting, I discovered several statistics that were quite alarming:

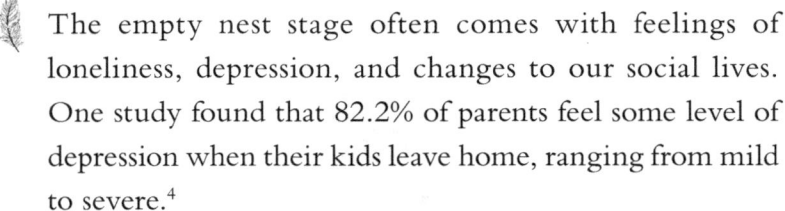

The empty nest stage often comes with feelings of loneliness, depression, and changes to our social lives. One study found that 82.2% of parents feel some level of depression when their kids leave home, ranging from mild to severe.[4]

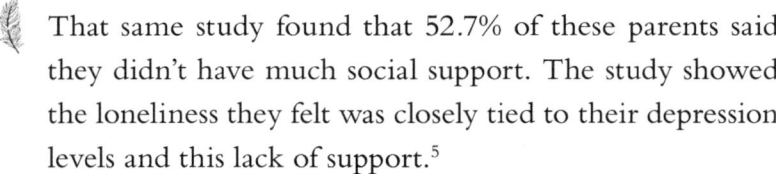

That same study found that 52.7% of these parents said they didn't have much social support. The study showed the loneliness they felt was closely tied to their depression levels and this lack of support.[5]

Psychologists say it can take up to two years to adjust to being an Empty Nester if you don't have a plan.[6]

In 2023, the US Surgeon General declared loneliness a public health epidemic in America.[7]

Too many parents are suffering unnecessarily and are often blindsided with the complex changes that come when their last child moves out. Loss of purpose, a quieter home, and upheaval in daily rituals can all wreak havoc on the best-intended new Empty Nester. My wish is to alleviate some of this pain. Let's shift our conversation about Empty Nesting from a position of lack to the potential for more joy. When your children are in high school, it's a great time to begin untethering yourself from the responsibilities your teenagers can now handle. Encourage them to take on tasks you once managed. It gives them fresh confidence and frees up more time to focus on yourself. The sooner you start to do this, the happier and healthier the transition will be for both of you when your child moves out on their own.

Today's parents have access to greater opportunities during this phase of life more so than previous generations. There has never been a more opportune moment to proactively prepare for what lies ahead while maintaining your happiness and health. But how do you do that? What is Empty Nest Syndrome, why does it affect millions of people, and what's the best way to avoid it?

Oxford Languages defines *Empty Nest Syndrome* as "sadness or emotional distress affecting parents whose children have grown up and left home."[8] It is important to note that Empty Nest Syndrome is not a medical or psychiatric health condition listed in the *Diagnostic and Statistical Manual of Mental Disorders, 5th edition.*[9] However, research does show that Empty Nest Syndrome can lead to mental health issues, such as depression and anxiety, or engaging in behaviors that can have a negative impact such as financial risk-taking or substance use disorders.[10]

Some parents adjust to their new roles as Empty Nesters within several months, but for others, it can take years, and not everyone experiences Empty Nest Syndrome the same way.[11] For example, your partner may seem fine while you end up having a very difficult time. Empty Nest Syndrome may differ in other cultures and countries with varying childcare arrangements, but in general, most cultures experience similar feelings.[12]

Listed below are some of the most common feelings associated with Empty Nest Syndrome[13]:

- **Grief**—deep sadness, possibly the five stages of grief: denial, anger, bargaining, depression, and acceptance.

- **Loneliness**—adrift, like a boat without a rudder, suddenly directionless, empty, and lacking purpose.

- **Mild depression**—loss of energy and motivation to do the things you used to do.

Fear and worry—uncertain and afraid of your life ahead, being preoccupied with your child's well-being.

 Loss of purpose—lack of meaning in your day-to-day life.

EBBING AND FLOWING

Empty Nesting can be a roller coaster full of highs and lows, with strong, overwhelming emotions hitting you at the weirdest times. For example, I was in the grocery store one day, and my eyes welled up with tears as I walked by my middle daughter's favorite snack, which I no longer needed to buy. Who knew a box of gluten-free crackers had so much power? Or sometimes I would peek into their clean, empty rooms and find myself longing for the beautiful, messy chaos that took place daily when they still lived under our roof.

This year we really felt the void of having two daughters away at college. We missed their energy, laughter, and presence in our everyday lives. And our youngest started driving, so the long days at home left me feeling lonely, bored, and without a purpose. The loneliness was palpable. I knew I had to find some type of work or passion project, and I know I'm not alone.

Chances are you feel this way, and that's why you bought this book. It's important to educate yourself on these symptoms so you can avoid some unnecessary pain. It took me a while to adjust when my second daughter moved out, but with time, compassion, and preparation, I discovered new ways to spend my days. I wrote my first book, started a business, and even made some new friends along the way. I'm maximizing my time with my youngest who is still at home while also nurturing some of my own dreams. Life is good, and I want that for you too.

On the bright side, several new Empty Nesters we know adapted rather quickly and are taking advantage of their newfound freedom. It's been inspiring to watch their journeys. We have friends currently RVing around the country and having a blast! Others are taking their dream vacations, one to Iceland and another to Italy with five other brand-new Empty Nesting couples.

How cool is that? Two of our friends created their dream businesses. One joined a pickleball league, and one is currently halfway around the world providing relief work to thousands of refugees. These are great examples of how to make the most

Find joy amidst the pain— look for the glimmers.

of your next chapter. Want to know why they were able to adjust so quickly? They prepared for it. Before their last one graduated, they crafted a vision, made incredible plans, and little shifts in their daily lives. It made all the difference in the world.

PROCEED WITH GRACE

Sometimes even with preparation, Empty Nesting hits parents hard, and it can take a little longer to find your groove again. That's okay. Be kind to yourself if you think this might happen to you. The tools provided throughout this book will help you immensely. One of the best ways to avoid Empty Nest Syndrome is to find joy amidst the pain. Acknowledge and accept they coexist. Just like in life, they will. My friend Kate reminds me to "look for the glimmers." They are always there if you seek them out.

As your children begin to move out, you will start to have more time to focus on yourself again. It may feel uncomfortable at first, but lean in and embrace it. Working on your goals and passion projects can be very fun, fulfilling, and much easier to do when you have fewer things pulling you in a million directions. If you work full-time, you too can find extra time to work on things you love to do, or maybe even discover a new career that you love even more than the one you have today. This is such a great time to make a change into a more passionate and purposeful work position! The change of pace when Empty Nesting arrives can take some getting used to for sure, but I promise you can and will find joy and purpose in this phase of life. It's time to start envisioning what you want to create for your next best chapter.

I'm so glad I took a leap of faith and started working on my first book when my second daughter moved out. I have learned so much about this very important topic and love helping mothers prepare for Empty Nesting a few years ahead of becoming one. My clients have a long list of things they want to do during their Empty Nesting years. They feel invigorated again!

Here's a sample of a few things they can't wait to do: go on adventures with their husbands, visit their children, do work that they love, climb to Mount Everest base camp, travel with other Empty Nesters, take cooking classes with friends, golf, ski, start business, and volunteer more often. The list goes on and on. It's truly inspiring.

By simply being aware of the changes coming and making a few adjustments, you can look forward to this next chapter of your life rather than dread it. With the right balance of self-care, reflection, preparation, and exploration, this next stage of your life can be so fulfilling. When my youngest child moves out, I will be back on that emotional roller coaster for sure. But this time around, I will be more prepared to enjoy the ups and downs. Even though I will miss her terribly, I now know I can thrive as an Empty Nester. And so can you.

Take time to reflect, recharge, and refocus before stepping into this new season of life. There's power in the pause. It is a great space to create from, and it's a perfect time to reground and recenter yourself so this next phase of life goes smoothly. Reflection is crucial for both your mental and emotional well-being. Momentarily hitting that Pause button on the busyness of everyday life can help you appreciate all that you have done as a mother. Motherhood is one of life's greatest joys, isn't it? I wish we all acknowledged and celebrated the countless mini miracles we have created for our families more often. They're magnificent.

Before you start to set new goals for yourself, let's take a minute and look back. Mothers often spend time reflecting solely on their children's accomplishments, but it's important to acknowledge your own as well. In short, you must look back before you move forward. I want *There's power in the pause.* to take you on a beautiful journey back to the beginning where it all started. I want you to reflect on when you first became a mother. The heartwarming moment when your younger self held your beautiful baby for the first time.

As you begin to look back, allow yourself the time to complete the following reflection exercise for Chapter 2 in your journal.

Chapter 2 Reflection Exercise

Find a special photo of you when you first became a mother. Whether it's one from the day your child was born or your first Mother's Day. Look at that precious picture, and really connect with that younger version of yourself.

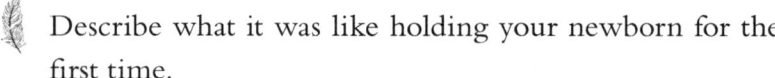 Describe what it was like holding your newborn for the first time.

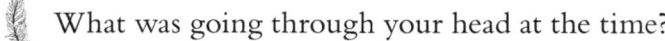 What was going through your head at the time?

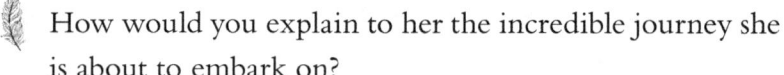 How would you explain to her the incredible journey she is about to embark on?

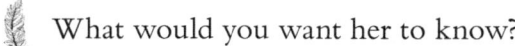 What would you want her to know?

After completing this exercise, I framed a photo from my first Mother's Day. It now resides on my desk where I can see it every day. I also reread my old journals. I loved remembering how I felt as a new mom, filled with so many hopes, wishes, and dreams I had for my new family.

My heart swelled with love and compassion as I started to reconnect with my younger self. She has so much on the road ahead of her, some she would be prepared for, some not. I wanted to reach through the picture, give her a hug and a few words of encouragement, and remind her to look for the glimmers every single day. There are so many. I decided I needed to write a letter to that new mom I once was from the mother I am today. This was such an impactful exercise for me, and I invite you to do the same.

You've come so far since the day you became a mother. It's now time to reflect on and take pleasure in the life you've so lovingly built for yourself and your family over the years. Take a minute to write her a letter and connect to your younger self.

To the young mother version of me . . .

 What kind of mother did you hope to be?
- *Tell your younger self what kind of mother you have become.*

 Can you believe how much you know now versus then?
- *Tell her how much you've learned to instill her with excitement, confidence, and faith for her future.*

 What scared you as a new mom?
- *Tell her how it all worked out or how you got through some difficult times because of her strength.*

 What were your dreams for your family?
- *Tell her about some of the incredible dreams that came true.*

 What would you want to tell her about her children and who they have become today?
- *Tell her about her amazing little humans that she gets to share her love, life, and wisdom with.*

 What kind of struggles were coming your way?
- *Tell her about a few bumps in the road and how she got through them with grit and grace.*

What's the most important thing you want to tell this younger version of yourself?

  o *Give her a "North Star nugget," one incredibly powerful thing she can hold on to forever.*

 Thank her for how she showed up every day, how much love she gave and continues to give, and how much she has grown as a woman.

 Forgive her for not being perfect (there's no such thing), and applaud her efforts to be the best mom she could be.

By writing this letter to your "beautiful, brand-new mother" version of yourself, you are bridging the gap between her dreams of yesterday and your present self. This reflection and introspection are reminders of the transformative power you possess and the immense strength you've carried through the ebbs and flows of motherhood.

It's a celebration of growth, resilience, and the unique, beautiful bond between a woman of yesterday and the extraordinary mother you are now. It's a testament to your powerful, unique journey.

Your Highlight Reel Time to Shine!

*Motherhood is a collection of countless small moments
that add up to a lifetime of love, sacrifice, and
joy. It's your beautiful, unique masterpiece.*

—UNKNOWN

I'm so glad you took time to write a letter to your younger self. When you're in the thick of raising kids, it's easy to get caught up in the hustle and bustle of life and forget how far you've come. Take a moment right now to pause, reflect, and honor all that you have done over approximately two decades. Can you believe how much you've grown and learned as a person in the process? Look at everything you have created for your beautiful family over the years—it's amazing! And the world has changed so much during this time too, so you should be extra proud of how you got here.

I can't help but pause and reflect on how vastly different life was back in 2001 when I became a mother. In those days, the absence of social media platforms such as YouTube, Facebook, Instagram, and TikTok meant that we couldn't simply look up whether a fever or rash was normal or how to make healthy baby food with just a few clicks.

Look at everything you have created for your beautiful family over the years—it's amazing!

Just now, I searched Pinterest for "healthy baby food recipes," and thousands of options popped up. Instead, navigating the intricacies of motherhood meant relying on traditional methods such as reading books, seeking advice from friends and family, and trusting your instincts. (Which often meant just winging it!) It was a time when parenting was shaped by personal interactions and the wisdom passed down through generations, creating a sense of community and shared experiences that feels increasingly rare nowadays.

In today's world, navigating parenthood during the social media boom presents unique challenges for both parents and children—one that our parents did not have to face. The constant pressure to measure up to idealized standards can be overwhelming at times unless you learn to turn down the volume or tune it out entirely.

Do you find yourself yearning for those simpler days when seeking parenting advice meant reaching out to a friend, asking a neighbor, or calling your mom? Despite some of the current challenges we all face, I hope looking back on your parenting years fills you up with a deep sense of pride. The contrast between then and now serves as a testament to your ability and resilience in facing the ever-evolving landscape of parenting in the modern world.

Can you imagine how it's going to change over the next twenty years? I can only guess! So let's take some time to quiet down the noise and highlight your favorite mom moments.

STEP INTO THE SPOTLIGHT

When was the last time you thought about your accomplishments since becoming a mother? You have been parenting now for close to two decades or more, and I bet you've rarely slowed down to think about what you are most proud of. All the beautiful little details you've delicately woven into your family's unique story are truly remarkable. You deserve to review and celebrate your incredible journey. Throughout the years, you've overcome and learned so much, so take a moment and marvel at all you have created and accomplished.

There's a great way to capture all this information. It's called a highlight reel, and you are going to create one for yourself in the next exercise. Highlight reels are used in sports all the time. It's when players take their best performances and compile them into a collection of memorable moments, summing up their greatest achievements. Every highlight reel includes what they've accomplished, their strengths as a player, and what they are most proud of.

> *All the beautiful little details you've delicately woven into your family's unique story are truly remarkable.*

Highlight reels can serve as a valuable feedback tool for Empty Nesters. It's great to look back at the last fifteen to twenty years before you make a game plan for the years ahead. You too can create your own highlight reel filled with your favorite moments, traditions, and experiences. This highlight reel not only celebrates your achievements and favorite memories, but it also showcases the beautiful legacy you have built for your family and the sacred imprints you have left on your children's hearts forever.

Reflecting on how far you have come in your personal journey holds extraordinary power. Power that can illuminate your incredible past and reveal new things you might want to do in your future. Reflection, like a timeless mirror, gives you the clarity to understand your true self and uncover the wisdom you have acquired through your experiences. It is in these moments of quiet contemplation that you can gain a profound understanding of who you were in the past, who you are today, and who you aspire to become in the future.

Take some time right now to create your own personal "Mom Highlight Reel." (And why has no one thought of this?!) Wouldn't that be an amazing gift to yourself? One minute you were holding a newborn, and now you have a young adult in your home, all in the blink of an eye. Give yourself time to reflect on and acknowledge all that you've done for your family. Let me give you examples of what two highlight reels could look like.

My dad had a long list of achievements in his lifetime. If you look at his résumé, he accomplished everything he set out to do. Flying airplanes was the true love of his life. He was an incredibly decorated pilot. Throughout his career, he worked for the Air Force, Boeing, and the Secret Service. He flew fifty different airplanes, logged tens of thousands of hours, experienced forty-three engine failures (six of which were single-engine airplanes), flew in three wars, and survived it all. Impressive, to say the least.

That is the highlight reel my dad would probably have given you. However, when I bring up my highlight reel for him, almost none of that shows up. Of course, I am proud of his accomplishments, but only a few of them would be on my list. Want to know what's at the top of my list for him? When I was younger, every weekend when he got home from a flying trip, he would take me to feed the ducks. We would sit on a bench at our favorite nearby pond tossing breadcrumbs into the water for hours, just talking and laughing our time away. He was completely present with me. He traveled a lot for work, so any time I could get with him meant a lot to me. If you know the insightful book *The Five Love Languages* by Gary Chapman, you will understand what I mean.[14] My love language is quality time. Sitting with my dad, not rushing anywhere, with zero interruptions, was priceless.

Afterward, we would go to our favorite restaurant, Lil' Jon in Bellevue, Washington. My brother and I still go there to this day. While we waited for our food, he would pull out a napkin and have me make a scribble on it. Within a minute or two, he could create these hilarious character drawings. I swear that man turned every squiggle into a masterpiece. I still have some of our napkins to this day, and I cherish them. My memories of those slow Sunday mornings might have made my dad's personal highlight reel as well. I will never know. But those hours he spent with me, just being with me, are some of my most favorite memories of all.

CELEBRATE YOUR CAPABILITIES

Spending time creating your highlight reel can give you a fresh sense of confidence, purpose, and self-worth. Your role as a mother extends beyond your day-to-day responsibilities. The impact you've made on your children is profound. Remembering the achievements, joys, and milestones you have reached as a mom reminds you of how capable you are and the significant influence you have in their lives.

It should also instill a belief in yourself that you can do it again. You can go create something amazing for yourself in this next phase of life. Writing down these memories helps you approach Empty Nesting with a heightened sense of fulfillment and a good dose of excitement. Knowing you have raised your children with love, dedication, and countless moments of joy is priceless.

Magical mini-moments make a lifetime of beautiful memories.

Magical mini moments make a lifetime of beautiful memories.

What would be on your highlight reel from your last two decades? What are the breadcrumbs you may have tossed into the water with your children along the way? What memories and ripple effects did those breadcrumbs leave? What would you have left off your list before I told you my duck story?

In your journal, it's time to create your highlight reel. Feel free to list your big, public accomplishments, but don't forget to highlight those magical mini moments you've created with your family along the way.

Chapter 3 Reflection Exercise

Write down as much as you can about your journey as a mother. Remember, don't focus on your kids' accomplishments right now. Yes, those are extremely important, but let's focus on you for a minute. I invite you to think about these questions as you put together your personal Mom Highlight Reel.

- What have you enjoyed most about raising your children?

- What are you most proud of?

- What memories pop into your head that are priceless?

- What memories make you laugh out loud?

- What have you learned?

- What have you personally overcome, and what did that teach your children?

- What environment did you create for your child to grow up in?

- What obstacles did you work through together, and how did this make your family stronger?

What values are most important to you?

 What are your best attributes as a mother?

None of us are perfect because there's no such thing as a perfect parent. As Maya Angelou is ascribed with saying, "Do the best you can until you know better. Then when you know better, do better."[15] If some not-so-perfect moments pop up, that's okay. They did for me too—totally normal. But keep in mind that your Mom Highlight Reel is supposed to focus on your best moments. It should make you proud of your life and how far you have come. Take time to write down all the good stuff.

This may take a while.

Spend some time going through pictures, albums, or any journals if you have them. Reminisce. Look how young your kids were. How young you were! And look at how far you've come. Take some time to enjoy this process because you deserve it. You've done such an amazing job with your little humans, and you need to know that on a soul level.

CHAPTER 4

Little Moments Are Big Moments
Make Time to Dance in the Rain

When you dance, your purpose is not to get to a certain place on the floor; it's to enjoy each step along the way.

—WAYNE DYER

I 'm so glad you took the time to create your Highlight Reel. I'm reaching through these pages and giving you the biggest hug and high five! If you would like to share something you loved about the process with our community, go to theemptynesterclub on all things social. We would love to hear from you!

I am currently writing this chapter in one of my favorite places on earth. It's my friend Karah's house in Coto de Caza, California. Four of my close friends and I have been getting together twice a year for the past ten years. We sit around her large kitchen table for several days catching up on life, kids, emails, etc. It's hard to explain, but after these weekends, I come home completely recharged, refreshed, and renewed. When my husband asks if we went out or did anything, I say, "No, we just sat around her kitchen table all day catching up on projects." He thinks we're nuts.

Our conversations go something like this:

Husband: "You mean you didn't go out to dinner or go to the beach or anything?"

Me: "Nope. We just sat around in our pajamas working on our computers, talking for hours, and walking outside for a bit, but that's about it."

Husband: *Gives me a blank stare, shrugs his shoulders, and leaves the room more confused than ever.*

These trips are the best because we spend uninterrupted girl time connecting with each other and working on our unique to-do lists. One of us is always scrapbooking; one is cleaning up their email inbox (guilty!); and the other three sort photos, fix technology issues, create invitations—stuff like that.

We share how our kids are doing, the highlights and the challenges. We talk about motherhood, marriage, family, you name it. And the best part is we get to eat cheese, drink wine, and stay in our pajamas almost all weekend long. It's an inexpensive trip, a drive or flight to a friend's house, and it's priceless. I highly recommend you invite three or four friends and plan your own trip. Immediately.

Years ago, we started giving each other little "happys" on these trips. "Happys" are small gifts that remind us how grateful we are for our friendships over the years. For example, my "happy" from Karah this trip is a beautiful clay turquoise heart that says "Dance" on it, which is so perfect because I'm writing my "Make Time to Dance in the Rain" chapter right now. Don't you just love the beautiful synchronicities in life?

PONDERING OUR PARENTING

On our last trip, we had several conversations about Empty Nesting. Each of us are at different stages in our parenting journey, but a few were right in the thick of becoming brand-new Empty Nesters. As our children leave the nest, it's natural to look back and hope we did the best job we possibly could.

We wondered if we taught them enough life skills and raised them to be kind, confident individuals. Are they ready for the world? Is the world ready for them? And will they ever remember to take the darn lint out of the dryer before it grows to the size of a football? These questions we asked ourselves were so normal; however, it baffles me what answers can bubble right to the surface.

The *perceived* mistakes.

Why do we sometimes get hung up and hyperfocus on a few "not so great" moments rather than acknowledge and celebrate the million little moments we got right? The significant and loving things we did for our families should always take center stage. This happened a bit while we each shared our stories about raising our kids. We cried, hugged, and talked through it, reminding each other that we are all loving mothers despite a few hiccup moments.

That's life.

We agreed that balancing motherhood with our many other responsibilities is an exciting, challenging, personal, and complex journey for each of us.

We also discussed the pressure that comes with being a mom in today's world. Society has created the most ridiculous, unachievable definition of what it means to be a "good mom." I don't even like the term "good mom." I mean, who sets that bar anyway? If you know who they are, I would like a word.

The expectations for mothers can be overwhelming and leave you feeling like you aren't doing enough, when in reality, you are doing just fine. Taking care of your children, yourself, your home, your pets, spending time with friends and family, working, cooking, volunteering, cleaning, earning a living, paying bills, and having anything left over for yourself or your partner is a lot. No wonder it's so hard to sleep through the night. Maybe it's not just menopause!

It's gotten out of control for our kids too. When you were a teenager, would you have survived the same multiple AP classes, extracurricular sports, homework, volunteering, work, testing, and college application process that your child goes through today? I would probably have cracked under all the pressure.

I find myself longing for the uncomplicated and carefree environment in which I grew up, particularly when compared to the immense pressure modern mothers and teens face today. The constant influence of social media and the relentless pursuit of ensuring our children achieve nothing short of academic and athletic excellence can be exhausting and out of alignment with what truly matters. Sometimes I find it hard to balance it all, and I know I'm not alone.

The expectations for mothers can be overwhelming and leave you feeling like you aren't doing enough, when in reality, you are doing just fine.

LET GO OF COMPARISON

You probably are someone who carries the weight of the world on your shoulders. Going forward, I would love for you to give yourself a break from time to time. Stop shaming and comparing yourself to others, okay? Enough already. Get comfortable defining what's right for you and your family based on what you want, not how society tells you it should be. There are so many ways to be a connected, present, and loving mom, so don't pigeonhole yourself into thinking it has to look a certain way.

It doesn't.

For years I ran Teacher Appreciation Day at our local elementary school and loved it. I have a soft spot for teachers because my mother and my two mothers-in-law were incredible teachers. Our team had fun spoiling the staff members, but something happened one year that I never forgot. Dozens of parents had signed up to make lunch, bring small gifts for the faculty, and decorate the classroom doors.

I was busy preparing our superhero-themed lunch, and in walked a mom I hadn't met yet. She was quiet, a bit shy, and looked a little down. She walked in and immediately started apologizing.

"I am so sorry I couldn't do more. I work, and my mom is ill. It's been stressful, and all I could do was sign up to bring these cups." A few tears slipped their way down her cheeks as she lowered her gaze and held out the plastic bag of cups. She was covered in that all-too-familiar self-imposed shame cloud.

I immediately stopped what I was doing, walked over, and gave her a hug. I looked her straight in the eye and said, "This is perfect. You are doing great. Thank you for signing up to help. Every bit matters."

We took a breath together.

A short pause.

I looked up and saw something familiar in her eyes. The struggle. The exhaustion. The shame. It occurred to me that sometimes we all need a little grace, a little pat on the back to remind ourselves we're doing okay. She looked as if a huge weight had been lifted off her shoulders.

We all need to slow down to give and receive more of these mini meaningful moments. To get clear on what really matters—connection.

In today's divided world, with countless distractions and ways to check out, it's time to check back in with yourself and make sure you are choosing what's important to you and your family. If that means being kind to yourself when you have a lot going on, good. Take a break from social media. Say no to things you can't or don't want to do. Prioritize your personal priorities, always. And give yourself some grace. It's okay to bring the paper cups and maybe even pass the baton. (Hint—the younger moms have more energy for this anyway.)

We all need to slow down to give and receive more of these mini meaningful moments.

PRESENCE IS PRICELESS

My mom is someone who had her work-life balance and priorities figured out early on. She is beautiful, funny, smart, and I admire her so much. She modeled for me at a young age what a balanced and fulfilling life looked like to her, and how important it was to nurture my own gifts along the way. I'm so grateful for her example of love and beauty. She is the gold standard I've tried to emulate, even though I found myself falling short from time to time.

When I was eleven, she became a successful art docent at our local museum, worked there for thirty years, and eventually became the docent president. Yet somehow, she still found time to be there for me. Always. She pursued personal joy and excellence while still maintaining a balanced family life. Amazing. Here is one example of what I loved about my mom growing up.

Back in the day, when I played soccer, my mom would come to my games, chat with other parents, and cheer me on. She would bring a ginormous Ziploc bag of sliced oranges for us to share with my team. At half time, for ten glorious minutes, my teammates and I feverishly sucked down as much juice as possible before being sent back into the game on a scorching hot gravel field. The good ol' days! There was no negotiating for a longer break because you were overheating. You knew you had to go back in and play your hardest with zero complaints.

Here's the gem in this:

She didn't define what kind of mother she was by bringing some viral treat with apples carved up to look like rainbows or rosebuds. My mom came to watch me play. She was present for me. I was so proud when I saw her cheering me on from the sidelines. I played better. My mom came to watch me, and that's what mattered.

That's what I believe our kids crave more than ever these days: the less stressed, undistracted, not-chasing-perfection-all-the-time version of ourselves. Sometimes it's hard to balance work, life, and family. I get it, but I do think it's a good reminder of what is important. Showing up for the ones we love and spending quality time with them is the best thing we can to do with our time.

Let me ask you this: How present do you feel today? We are constantly distracted and being pulled in a million different directions—whether it's with work, school, volunteering, personal commitments, etc. I have worked hard over the past few years to stay more present, say no more often to things that don't serve me, and say yes to things that truly matter. Stopping to identify who and what are doing the pulling in your life can be so valuable. Once I turned fifty, I started to ask myself

Say yes to things that truly matter.

this important question more often: "Why am I giving away so much of my energy to this person, place, or thing that doesn't fill me up when I could be putting that same energy into what matters to me or someone that I actually matter to?"

Let us always strive to create meaningful moments with our children, even in the smallest ways. We have the power to impact our children in ways they will remember for a lifetime, and this doesn't end when they move out of the house.

The next reflection exercise really helped me know in my heart that we've made so many great family memories over the years, and we will make wonderful new memories in our future. It will just look a little different than before. I hope you enjoy this exercise as much as I did.

You've done so much for your family. You've crafted countless cherished memories for them, and now it's time to hear their perspective. Who could better recount

We have the power to impact our children in ways they will remember for a lifetime, and this doesn't end when they move out of the house.

the magic you've created as a mom than your own children?

Get ready for your next exercise—and keep the tissue box handy!

Chapter 4 Reflection Exercise

Chat with your children to uncover some of their favorite memories of you and what truly matters to them. However old they are, ask them. Just like my story about my dad's highlight reel (the first one) and my highlight reel for him (the second one with the ducks), do the same with your children.

Here are some prompts you could use when talking to your children. Even better? Have them write down their answers so you can save them forever. My incredible editor and all things amazing, Tracy, did this right after she started working on my book. Her grown boys took two weeks to write down their answers and gave them to her on Mother's Day. They are now hanging in her office. She says reading their responses helped her see herself through their eyes, and it was incredibly encouraging. Their favorite memories were when she was just being herself! What a wonderful gift.

Feel free to come up with your own questions as well. Make sure to record their answers in some way so you can keep them forever.

 What's one of your favorite planned or unplanned memories of us together?

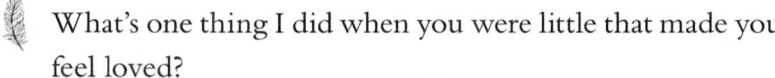

What's one thing I did when you were little that made you feel loved?

What's your favorite family tradition?

What's one thing I do that makes you laugh?

What's your favorite meal I make?

What's your favorite thing we have done and continue to do together?

What's one thing you love we did together that you think I might not remember?

What's one of the best things I have taught you?

What do you love most about me?

Although it might be hard, try not to guide their answers with your memories. Let them come up with answers on their own. Avoid saying things like, "Don't you remember all those times I drove you to practice?" or "What about when I always made your favorite homemade cookies for road trips?" I promise you, they remember those things too, but you want to hear their highlight reel about you, not yours. It's often amazing what pops into their heads. Whatever they share with you, please know those are core memories for them, and they're very special.

When I did this exercise with my three daughters, my middle daughter's answer to the first question surprised me. She said:

Mom, do you remember when I was twelve, and you were going through breast cancer? One afternoon we were in the kitchen, and it started to rain. You grabbed my hand and said, "Let's go outside and dance in the rain!" I was shocked! But then I laughed and said, "Why not?" And off we went to go dance in the rain. We held our hands up to the sky, laughing and twirling each other around while catching raindrops in our mouths. We were soaking it all up, Mom. It was great.

Writing this brings tears to my eyes. While I was recovering from breast cancer, I made a promise to myself that when I felt good, I was going to be as present as possible for my family. The effects of chemo and radiation didn't always make this easy, so I did my best to appreciate the in-between moments. The glimmers.

And guess what?

That one spontaneous choice turned into one of her favorite memories. I had completely forgotten about that until she told me. It made me remember so many other magical mini moments, so I went back and added them to my highlight reel, and I invite you to do the same.

Note: They also might come back with some funny stuff. Don't think mine were all sunshine and roses. Far from it. Right after she sent me that beautiful response, her next text to me said this:

Mom, do you also remember when I was four, we went to the mall, and you lost me for like ten minutes? You were crying and searching all over for me with the mall cop and ran into a college friend you hadn't seen in years. You said she looked at you like you were the worst mom ever! Ha! That's hilarious!

Touché, Riley, touché! I digress. Ah, the joys of motherhood. Your love for them has been unwavering, and it will continue as they embark on their own journey. Remember, you will always be their mother. Pause for a moment and really take in how much you've inspired and influenced your kids over the years with your endless love, humor, kindness, and compassion. It truly is remarkable.

CHAPTER 5

Your Toolbox

Out with the Old, in with the New

*Without letting go of the old, it is impossible
to make room for the new.*

—DEEPAK CHOPRA

Highlight reels are so special to have as you start planning for your Empty Nest years. Hopefully, you received some beautiful insight and feedback from your kids to hold close to your heart forever. What you've done for your family is incredible, and the impact you've had on your children is priceless. Every diaper you changed, every lunch you packed, every practice or performance you were running late for (but still made!), every meal you cooked, every load of laundry, every word of encouragement you gave, and every kiss good night— it all mattered. It always will. You've built a beautiful legacy for your family filled with so much love, fun memories, and incredible traditions.

Nice job, mama.

Empty Nesting is getting closer and closer, and it's important you put some time and energy back into yourself. As moms, sometimes we can get so busy and forget to assess how we're doing on an emotional, mental, spiritual, and physical level.

Let's do some internal housekeeping, or "soul-keeping" as I like to call it, to better understand how you've been showing up in your everyday life.

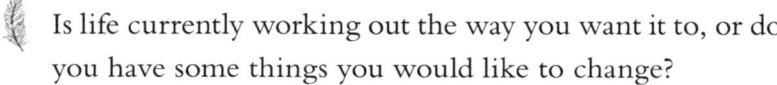 Is life currently working out the way you want it to, or do you have some things you would like to change?

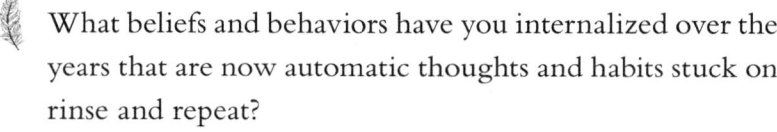 What beliefs and behaviors have you internalized over the years that are now automatic thoughts and habits stuck on rinse and repeat?

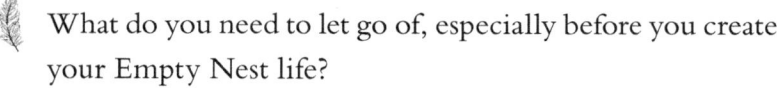 What do you need to let go of, especially before you create your Empty Nest life?

REVIEW YOUR TOOLS

There is a lot of science behind this, but first, let's address what I like to call your old toolbox. We need to assess if your go-to "tools" are working for you in a positive and uplifting manner or not. Some tools you have may be working well, and some might be holding you back. Let's define and refine them before you head into your Empty Nesting years. It's time for a little tune-up.

When I took myself through this next exercise, I was happy with most of the tools I was using. However, I discovered one crippling tool that needed to go—my muscle for always putting everyone else's needs ahead of my own. It is a well-developed coping mechanism that runs deep, and one I learned at a very young age.

When I was growing up, it was much safer to stay in the shadows and play small versus being in the spotlight. I deflected any praise for achievements I earned because I didn't feel worthy of winning. Being first felt very uncomfortable. I was constantly outwardly focused, doing anything for anyone at almost any cost. I'll never forget when in my mid thirties, I even had one woman tell me, "Wow, you have a beautiful voice and a powerful soul. Be careful with your gifts. You might not want to shine your light *too* brightly!"

Isn't that sad?

I went on to carry that belief within me for years, and I stopped singing—one of my favorite ways to express myself. Music has been one of my biggest soul whispers since I was a five-year-old, singing my first solo in front of my kindergarten class, complete with a rockin' red cowgirl outfit. They loved it, I loved it, and I never forgot the feeling of that day. It was magical. Singing had me at hello. And yet, I buried that gift for so long because of one person's opinion, which probably had more to do with her than me.

Hiding behind other people's success and dreams always felt safer to me. It still does, but I've realized it isn't fair to do this to myself anymore. I can no longer dim my light to brighten others' all the time. I have mastered the art of enthusiastically and effectively helping others achieve whatever they want to accomplish. Their dreams became my dreams. However, today I am working on turning some of that love and support back onto myself. It's a much more balanced and fulfilling way to live.

Don't get me wrong—I absolutely love to support my friends and family and see them winning at this game we call life. It's one of my greatest joys, but I wasn't doing any of this for myself. It's been a big problem for a long time. I realize now I should have been nurturing my own dreams alongside everyone else's. That's on me, and it's my responsibility to fix, but it's an old tool I am not bringing into my Empty Nesting years. I want to cheer everyone on, including myself, and help other recovering people-pleasers do the same.

Be honest with yourself. Think about where you are stuck on repeat. For example, saying yes to things you don't want to do. Or not acting on something you clearly do want to do because you are afraid to fail. Maybe you've been wanting to take better care of yourself, work out more, drink less, learn a new skill, be more patient, or invest in friendships that will fill you up rather than the ones that leave you feeling deflated.

It's easy to hide behind your hectic schedule when you're busy taking care of the kids. But soon that will change, and it'll be time to face reality. Some of these old tools in your toolbox just need to go. What once served a purpose in your life might be the very thing blocking you from feeling more fulfilled today.

Visualize your old toolbox. Is it weathered down and rusty, or are you happy with the tools you have inside? If you're happy with most of them, that's great! I was about fifty-fifty and knew I could do much better. Power tools—unlike old, self-deprecating rusty tools—are supposed to make you feel empowered. They equip you with the strength you need to speak your voice, stand in your truth, and create the future you want.

Gradually, over time, I had set aside some of my power tools, and unfortunately, I began to pick up a bunch of "I will compromise myself" tools instead. Tools such as, "I'm not worth it," and "What I want doesn't matter" were being used far too often in my life. When I took myself through this exercise, I didn't beat myself up, but I knew I had some major cleaning up to do. Maybe you can relate.

I think this happens to people slowly over time. You don't even notice it because they are gradual shifts you make in your small, day-to-day life choices. However, choosing what others want instead of what you want time and time again starts to leave little micro tears in your soul. It eventually becomes part of your identity and can leave you feeling resentful, restless, and unfulfilled.

> *"Fill up your own cup, and let them fall in love with the overflow."*

Think of it this way. Every time you say yes to something you don't want to do, you are saying no to something that better aligns with your values. A better way to live would be to "Fill up your own cup, and let them fall in love with the overflow," as Harry Styles so beautifully said.[16]

EMBRACE YOUR UNIQUENESS

Recently, I've learned from my brilliant therapist, Debra, that playing small is an inner childhood trauma response. We are unpacking it from all angles to better understand this behavior. There were payoffs for remaining small, like being able to hide, having excuses not to go 100 percent all in, or believing I would be safer if I didn't shine. This isn't true for me, and it's not true for you.

I'm doing a lot of reframing and rebuilding around this, and I must admit it's hard work, but so worth it. I am slowly becoming comfortable with who I am and allowing myself to shine too, no matter what other people say or think. I enjoy sharing my gifts with the world, and it feels good to be back in the sun with my inside light turned back on. I'm happy I feel so grounded in who I am before I become an Empty Nester.

So many middle-aged mothers are awakening to their individuality, finding their true voice, and rediscovering their unique passions and purpose. They don't care anymore about fitting in with the wrong people, places, or things and instead find themselves seeking out those that make them feel good just as they are. They want to fill their time with things that they love to do, not what other people expect them to do.

Nothing makes me happier than when someone comes up to me and shares how my book or course impacted their life. One reader said, "I read your book, and it helped me pick the One Thing I have wanted to do for thirty years but never made time for. And now I'm actually doing it! I spend time each day doing things that bring me joy without asking anyone's permission. I'm a new person!"

So many middle-aged mothers are awakening to their individuality, finding their true voice, and rediscovering their unique passion and purpose.

It's an incredible feeling to witness people finding their spark again.

Author Brené Brown shared something about this very topic on her socials, and it really stuck with me. Her choice of words are so insightful, intelligent, intentional, and just pure perfection! I would love to have dinner with her someday. She said:

Fitting in often implies conforming, or shaping yourself to align with the expectations, norms, and standards of others. It involves making personal adjustments, whether in behavior, attitudes, or even beliefs, to ensure acceptance or to avoid discomfort or rejection. Fitting in can often mean suppressing one's uniqueness or authenticity to meet the group's standard. True belonging, on the other hand, is grounded in authenticity and self-acceptance. It is when individuals are embraced and valued for who they are, rather than how well they meet a preset standard or norm.

Her great advice reminds me of that old Dr. Seuss quote: "Why fit in when you were born to stand out?"[17] This is such a good reminder for you to embrace your uniqueness and never play small for anyone. It's time to show up as your best authentic self, no matter what that looks like. Stop shrinking your puzzle piece to fit into everyone else's puzzle. Take up space. Embrace it. Own your uniqueness. There's room at the table for everyone and their gifts, yours included.

UPGRADE YOUR TOOLS

Debra and I came up with this anchoring statement, and maybe it can help you too. When I start to feel that all-too-familiar pull to drop everything I'm doing for what someone else wants or needs right away, I pause and remind myself of my new contract with myself: "*I will never again abandon myself for another person because what matters to me*

Own your uniqueness.

matters." Now, before I say yes to something, I ask myself these two questions:

 Do I want to say yes to this opportunity?

 What am I giving up in order to do it?

If it aligns with me, great. If not, it's a big, fat no.

In order to feel comfortable saying no, your yes has to be bigger. As mothers, we all have a well-developed muscle of setting our needs aside because we love our families and there's always so much to do.

But let me gently remind you of something. When the kids move out and your daily rhythm changes, if you've been hiding behind your busyness like I was, the jig is up. You are going to run out of places to hide. You'll end up right smack in front of your soul whispers and, as we age, they are harder to ignore. It's time to bring them to life.

It seems so easy at first, but new habits and behaviors can be uncomfortable. Letting go of how you've been showing up for a long time can be both exhilarating and downright painful! It's time to let go of some old habits and behaviors and lean into new, stronger, more aligned ones that you are going to create for yourself right now. Change can be challenging and difficult to maintain if you don't teach your brain to get comfortable using some of your new tools. Here's one way you can do that.

In his book *The Power of Habit*, author Charles Duhigg explores the science behind habits and how they shape our lives.[18] One key concept is how the brain forms habits to be efficient and follow familiar pathways. This makes it difficult for people to let go of old behaviors and ways of being to embrace new ones.

By bringing awareness to these ingrained habits, individuals can start by identifying their habit loops: the cues, routines, and rewards that drive their behaviors. Understanding your triggers can help you consciously begin to interrupt those old patterns and replace them with new, positive behaviors.

This could involve creating a new morning routine and reinforcing it with consistent rewards to make your new habit more appealing and comfortable. Or you could simply start charging your phone in your bathroom so it's not by your bed, making it more inconvenient when you feel like mindlessly scrolling on social media. Over time, this process can help rewire your brain and establish healthier, more productive patterns of behavior. We will discuss these concepts more in depth in chapter 16. I'm glad you are looking at your toolbox now in case you have some work to do like I did. I could not continue to betray myself anymore, and if you are doing this too, I hope you choose to make some changes like I did. It was hard work but extremely worth it.

It took me until my fifties to learn that I can't twist and contort myself in order to please everyone all the time, and I shouldn't be doing that anyway. My choices and where I spend my time need to align with myself, my friends, and my family. Peace and happiness are now two top priorities for me, and I want the same for you. In case your priorities are a little misaligned too, let's get you charged up so you can define your amazing new power tools and feel strong enough to set aside your not-so-great ones.

Chapter 5 Reflection Exercise

As you continue to replace negative behaviors with more positive ones, your new habits will start to take over as the old ones fade away. It's an empowering and uplifting experience that feels so good. And the best part is these positive changes will have a ripple effect in every area of your life.

Let's reorganize your toolbox.

Start with the easy part: What needs to go? I invite you to make a list of every tool that no longer serves you and take it out of your toolbox. This isn't a time for blaming or shaming yourself for those old, not-so-great tools. We all have tools that need to go.

Create a list noting which tools you are tossing out and why. Knowing *why* something no longer serves you will help you never pick up that old tool again. Examples of this could be:

When using my old tools, I would . . .

 Shut down instead of speak up when someone was being rude to me.

 Frequently break promises to myself.

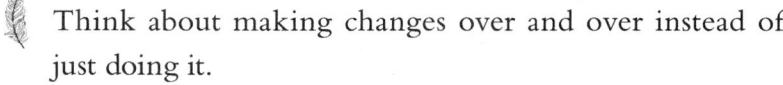

Think about making changes over and over instead of just doing it.

Focus on the possible negative outcomes versus a positive one.

Overworry a lot.

Feel unworthy of doing something solely for myself.

Next, envision your brand-new toolbox.

It's beautiful and shiny with no marks on it. It hasn't felt the weight of pain or disappointment. It contains nothing except what you're about to put into it. What tools are you going to keep that are currently working well, and what brand-new tools are you going to put into this toolbox that you've never even used before?

This is the toolbox you will be taking into your future, so think big. Your brain will seek out what you focus on. If you're having trouble thinking of some new power tools, think of people you love and the qualities you admire about them. Write those down. Chances are those are tools you want to develop in yourself, so add them to your toolbox.

Here is a list of tools I am going to keep. When . . .

I'm angry, I remain patient.

Someone needs help, I'm there.

I'm tired, I still make time for my family.

Friends need someone to listen to, I hold space for them and don't give advice unless asked.

I miss a goal, I readjust and keep moving forward.

With my new tools, I . . .

Keep my promises to myself.

Am more present for my friends and family.

Validate myself internally rather than looking externally for validation.

Say yes when I mean yes and no when I mean no.

Choose courage over fear every time.

Taking time now to assess what is and isn't working for you will have a great impact on your next chapter. Empty Nesting can be viewed as a fresh start. It's a great time to check in with yourself and intentionally identify what you want more or less of in life.

When you start to replace your old tools with some new ones, that's when your brain might try to trick you into returning back to your original state. That's just the brain doing its thing. When this happens—and it will—do these four things immediately so you don't return to your old habit loop. Recognize. Acknowledge. Replace. Repeat.

Recognize that the old behavior resurfaced.

Acknowledge why it showed up.

Replace it with something out of your new toolbox.

 Repeat. Repeat. Repeat

Now, let's put your new tools to work!

CHAPTER 6

The Payoff of Courage vs. the Price of Regret
It's Time to Get into the Arena

Life shrinks or expands in proportion to one's courage.

—ANAIS NIN

Looking back, one of my greatest regrets I have in life was when I took long, unnecessary breaks from nurturing my passion for singing and songwriting. I took voice lessons with one of the best vocal coaches in Seattle, sang in my college choir, and wrote hundreds of lyrics and songs I've done absolutely nothing with.

I wish I had taken time to figure out how to juggle school, parenting, work, and still develop my love for music. Heck, even eighteen minutes a day adds up to over one hundred hours a year! I try to keep this statistic in my mind now when I'm starting any new endeavor. It would have been a nice hobby for me to consistently cultivate over the years.

My husband happens to be a great singer, guitar player, and band leader. He has been nurturing his craft for decades, even while our kids were young. I have zero excuses as to why I didn't learn right alongside him. (He's actually playing guitar right now. How funny is that? "Everlong" by the Foo Fighters— the best!)

He has always been way better at balance than me. I am disappointed that for years at a time, I shut down that part of myself for no real reason other than I didn't make it a priority. However, one time, one of my soul whispers nudged me in just the right way so that I finally listened, gave in to it, and took action. It was time. I was going to be brave and use some of my courage, just like the beloved lion in *The Wizard of Oz*, and go for a goal I had only ever dreamed about.

It was 2011, and the *X Factor* show was coming to Seattle. I decided to try out at the last minute, along with fifty-five thousand other hopefuls. I filled up my tank with gas and drove to the arena, not knowing how to get in or which songs to sing. When I got there, self-doubt started creeping in big time. My heart was racing, and my palms were a bit sweaty. Typical, right?

My inner critic was having a field day. The parking lot was jam-packed, and all I wanted to do was turn around and go home. Instead, I said to myself, "Okay, if a parking space is available, I will stay." Two seconds later, someone pulled out right in front of the stadium. First sign. Then I realized I would need a way to practice my songs while waiting in line for hours. My next thought was, "Okay, if I can find some headphones, I'll stay." Clearly, I was bargaining with the universe and my inner critic. There were no headphones in my car, but I kid you not, when I opened the driver's side door, right down on the ground was a pair of white plastic headphones. Sign number 2! The universe was clearly telling me, "You can do this. I got you! Go have fun and be courageous."

And so I did. *Roar.*

I was assigned a personal name tag with a number and label. There was *T* for "Teen," *A* for "Adult," and *O* for . . . I have no idea. *Odd? Other? Old?* Then I was given a ticket that told me where to sit and wait until my audition time: section 121, row 21, seat 1. The number 21 has always been a number in my life that shows up with blaring sirens from the universe saying I'm on the right path. I nervously sat for hours waiting for my turn as my inner critic was hard at work, giving me a million reasons to call it quits and leave.

Let's chat a little bit more about that.

When you choose to do something new, your inner critic will pop up because it's trying to keep you safe. As we talked about earlier, trying new things scares the brain, so it does anything and everything to stop you. I've given a name to my inner critic. Want to know what it is? It's a very unique and endearing name and describes my negative inner voice perfectly. I call mine the Itty-Bitty Shitty Committee.

Unfortunately, my inner critic is not just one internal voice trying to make me play small and run from great opportunities. It's an entire team of loud, obnoxious characters trying to get me to constantly live in fear and self-doubt instead of trusting my gut and stepping up with courage. Sound familiar? I have listened to my inner critics for years. They need to be fired and replaced, immediately. Okay, back to the audition.

NEXT-LEVEL COURAGE

There were about seventy-five audition booths in total. The heavy, dark-blue velvet curtains were draped open slightly so you could see into a few of them and watch the auditions. Thousands of contestants sang their hearts out to their assigned judge, and almost everyone was sent home. And some of them were really incredible! This one particular judge, I will call him Mr. Grinch, had been sending talented singers home all day long. One after the other. Kicking them to the curb like a piece of garbage. I was so relieved when after six hours of waiting, my turn finally came to audition, and I did not get assigned to him. Whew!

I sang my first song for my "less Grinchy" judge, and he asked to hear my second one. I thought, "Take a breath, that's a good sign, and just sing." At the end of my second song, the judge smiled, reached around into his briefcase, and handed me a Golden Ticket! I could not believe what was happening! I was stunned and so incredibly happy. I shook with disbelief. It had been years since I had allowed myself to sing out loud. This was a huge win for me. One of my soul whispers had been freed and allowed to soar, no matter what the outcome. The outcome didn't matter. Taking action did. A priceless payoff for a moment of courage.

I was proud I stuck it out and didn't bail. Showing up, being brave, and doing something I had wanted to do for decades was a huge win. Take that, Itty-Bitty Shitty Committee! I love music and had always wanted to experience the show in some capacity. If I had left, I would have missed out on the amazing gift I was given that day. Only a fraction of the people who tried out made it to the next round, and I was over the moon to be one of them.

The rest of that story is that I didn't make it to the TV rounds, but that's not the point. My second audition was the next morning, on June the twenty-first (another 21), in a small Seattle hotel room with two judges. Judge 1 was a woman with an incredible background in the music industry. And guess who I got for my second judge? Yep, you guessed it. Out of seventy-five judges, I got Mr. Grinch. Unbelievable. After singing my heart out for them, the woman wanted to send me through to the TV rounds. I was

> *Fear is just your creativity working in the wrong direction and it's easy to turn around when you listen to your heart.*

so excited! She tried convincing him; however, Mr. Grinch sat there deep in thought, discussed a few things with her, scrunched up his face, and said no. His word beat out hers. (Cue song . . . "You're a Mean One, Mr. Grinch.") Turns out his heart was three sizes too small.

Moral of the story: I was so thrilled I got to try out for this show and wasn't going to let one person's opinion of me change how I felt about how I did that day. I had chosen to be courageous and unlock one of my soul whispers that had been hidden away for years: singing. I now have a framed picture hanging in my office of me holding the Golden Ticket, reminding me to choose courage over fear every day—to leave breadcrumbs of bravery for my children to witness. Nike got it right: "Just Do It!"

Fear is just your creativity working in the wrong direction, but it's easy to turn around when you listen to your heart. I learned a lot from that experience and made a core memory for myself. No, I didn't even come close to winning the *X Factor*, but that's not the point.

Life rewards you for being brave and stepping into the arena. You just never know what might happen. What if I hadn't gone to the audition? Or received the Golden Ticket? Or had my singing validated by two, almost three, professional judges? Well, I think I would have always wondered over the years what could have been.

Life rewards you for being brave and stepping into the arena.

It wasn't about winning; it was about having courage to put myself out there.

My dad gave me a copy of this well-known speech years ago, and it hangs in my office next to my Golden Ticket. It's such an incredible reminder for us all to be courageous, step up, and do our best.

The Man in the Arena

It is not the critic who counts; not the man who points out how the strong man stumbles, or where the doer of deeds could have done them better. The credit belongs to the man who is actually in the arena, whose face is marred by dust and sweat and blood; who strives valiantly; who errs, who comes short again and again, because there is no effort without error and shortcoming; but who does actually strive to do the deeds; who knows great enthusiasms, the great devotions; who spends himself in a worthy cause; who at the best knows in the end the triumph of high achievement, and who at the worst, if he fails, at least fails while daring greatly, so that his place shall never be with those cold and timid souls who neither know victory nor defeat.

—THEODORE ROOSEVELT
at Sorbonne, Paris, France, on April 23, 1910[19]

ALLOW YOUR COURAGE TO COMMENCE

Your soul whispers never go away, and I hope by telling you this story, it made you think of a few of your own. Soul whispers can get muted and change over the years, but most of the time, they don't. They will keep trying to surface, begging to be heard. They live and breathe within you every day. They want to become a part of your life.

Things we have been drawn to since childhood are still deep wishes and dreams within us, and Empty Nesting is the perfect time to start listening to them again. Each of us has been called to do something special on this earth, and your soul knows what that is. It's time to turn up the dial on being courageous so you don't have to live with costly regrets in your Empty Nest years. We want your Empty Nest to be your fulfilling best.

In Bronnie Ware's groundbreaking book, *Top Five Regrets of the Dying: A Life Transformed by the Dearly Departed*, she illuminates the transformative power of self-reflection and the profound wisdom that lies in embracing our past experiences. Conducting over one thousand interviews with people on their deathbeds, here's what their top five regrets were in the form of wishes. They all said, "I wish . . .

5. I would have let myself be happier."
4. I would have expressed how I truly felt."
3. I would have stayed in touch with friends."
2. I wish I hadn't worked so hard."
1. And the top wish of the dying was, "I wish I had the courage to live a life truer to myself, not the life others expected of me."[20]

If the lessons in this book can teach us one thing, it's time to make some room for your soul whispers and what matters to you.

One of my lifelong best friends just reignited one of her soul whispers. She owns an incredible design services company called Sweet Pea Ink Creative (shameless plug). Their tagline is "Sweet yet spicy, bold yet refined. Whoever said you can't have it all clearly never met YOU." How awesome is that?

A lot of what you see on theemptynesterclub.com is her genius at work. We've known each other since we were twelve, and she gets my soul whispers. Even when I don't. She's never been happier and says it feels so good to be creating again. It has breathed new life back into her Empty Nesting days. All because she had the courage to pick up her gifts again.

Another incredible example of an Empty Nester choosing courage over fear is author Terry Sidford. She is a TEDx speaker, podcast host, professional coach, and author of two incredible soul-searching books about courage. She's a dear friend of mine who inspired me to become a writer and lives a truly inspirational courageous life.

It's time to make room for your soul whispers.

In her latest book, *Truth, Courage Love*, she talks about the power of courage and what is possible when you step into your greatness.[21] The secret is believing in what is possible for yourself and taking courageous action toward your unique goals. She innately knows on a soul level we are all capable of unlimited possibilities.

When her children left home, she began to pursue her passions wholeheartedly. It was scary at first and required her to step into the unknown. She felt out of her comfort zone but did it anyway. What happened on the other side of her fear was that she accomplished things she never thought possible.

She was finally doing for herself what she believed was possible for others. As Gay Hendricks calls it, she was in her "genius zone."[22] Once Terry had the courage to listen to her inner compass and take action, she became a best-selling author, TEDx speaker, podcast host, and international coach—all within three years' time!

In Terry's book, she says,

> Courage is from the Latin word *Cor*, meaning heart. Our strength comes from our heart and our Inner Compass. Courage allows you to face fear, connect to your heart, and lead you to that whisper inside that says, I know this is your calling or purpose in life. You will see what your heart knows when you quiet the noise that tells you anything different. It will guide you to living your best, most authentic life. When we live to our full potential, we change ourselves and everyone around us. We are a powerful ripple effect that can change the world. We all need to show up fully and live the life we are meant to live.[23]

Your Empty Nest chapter is a great time to listen to your heart, lean into your desires, and use some of your new tools with confidence and courage.

Tune into your inner voice, trust your instincts, and define your next chapter with courage.

I want you to go into this next phase with a well-crafted game plan for your tomorrows and no regrets of your yesterdays.

As your kids start to leave the nest, it's important for you to explore what lies ahead, define where you wish to invest your time, and discover how you can turn your dreams into a reality. Tune into your inner voice, trust your instincts, and define your next chapter with courage.

Chapter 6 Reflection Exercise

Reflecting on the payoff of courage versus the price of regret can be a transformative exercise. Choosing courage consistently over time can have a profound impact on all areas of your life, as it compounds with each act of bravery. It sets you on a path of growth, resilience, and fulfillment. Take a moment to write down your answers to these questions:

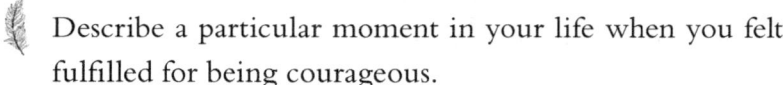 Describe a particular moment in your life when you felt fulfilled for being courageous.

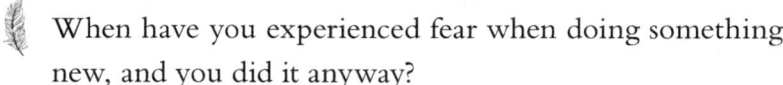 When have you experienced fear when doing something new, and you did it anyway?

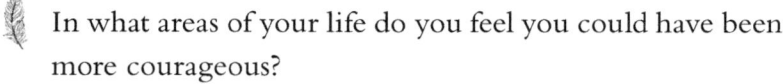 In what areas of your life do you feel you could have been more courageous?

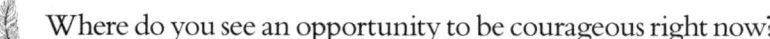 Where do you see an opportunity to be courageous right now?

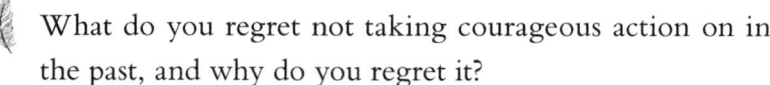 What do you regret not taking courageous action on in the past, and why do you regret it?

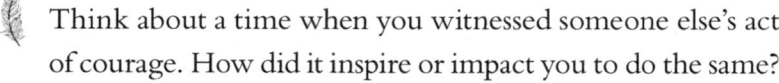 Think about a time when you witnessed someone else's act of courage. How did it inspire or impact you to do the same?

Take a moment to review your answers and embrace the lessons they hold. For in the end, one true measure of our worth lies not in the absence of fear but in the courage we choose to act on.

Accept That Change Is Coming Empty Nesting Is Right Around the Corner

Step into the new story you are willing to create.

—OPRAH WINFREY

No matter what stage in life you are in right now with your children, trust me, it goes by quickly. That sounds so cliché, but it's true. When this book hits the market, my youngest daughter will be starting her senior year in high school. How the heck did that happen so fast?

Whether your kids have already moved out, are beginning to move out, or you still have a few years before you even need to think about it, the time is going to fly by. Someday your kids will be out on their own living their lives, just like when you moved out of your parents' home ages ago. So it's best to just accept the fact that someday will be here. Soon.

In her book *The Gifts of Imperfection*, author Brené Brown (who I believe is a brand-new Empty Nester herself; if you know her, please send her my love . . . and my book!) emphasizes the significance of radical acceptance as a transformative practice.[24] According to Brown, radical acceptance involves acknowledging our vulnerabilities without judgment or shame.

When facing a big change, like an Empty Nest, she encourages individuals to lean into their feelings and embrace the uncertainty that comes with change. She emphasizes the importance of being open to the experience, allowing oneself to feel the emotions that arise, and being compassionate with yourself throughout the process. Brown advocates that self-compassion can cultivate a sense of resilience by acknowledging and accepting our vulnerabilities rather than trying to numb or avoid them. Such great advice to take into your Empty Nesting years.

EMBRACE YOUR EMOTIONS

Once I started acknowledging my own feelings of worry and sadness regarding my kids moving out, through radical yet gentle acceptance, my entire perception of the situation transformed for the better. I was able to flip my perspective. I now look at Empty Nesting not just as a period of intense change but also as an opportunity of growth for me. I can now lean into how excited my children are to start their adult lives and make their own mark in the world, while investing time into creative projects for myself. It's a win-win for everyone.

There's so much power in accepting your reality. It will empower you to handle this change more gracefully. True acceptance is the practice of fully and completely accepting reality as is, without judgment, resistance, or avoidance. It involves acknowledging and embracing the truth of a situation, even if it's challenging or unknown.

When it comes to Empty Nesting and facing the fact that your children will be moving out soon, acceptance can play a transformative role in your emotional well-being and adjustment to the future. Numerous studies highlight the positive effects of acceptance and mindfulness practices on overall well-being and mental health.[25] By practicing acceptance, Empty Nesters can experience the following benefits:

> *There's so much power in accepting your reality.*

 Improved emotional resilience

 Enhanced self-awareness

 Strengthened relationships

Freedom and empowerment

Accepting the upcoming changes allows you to reduce feelings of denial, process emotions more effectively, and bounce back more readily during this life transition. Introspection and self-reflection can give you a deeper understanding of your own identity, desires, and goals beyond the role of parenting. Adding gentleness while you go through this process is so important too. The life you've been living for approximately twenty years is about to change. So be gentle and kind with yourself as you begin to plan how to navigate these new waters.

WELCOME NEW OPPORTUNITIES

Empty nesting, though it may initially seem challenging to fully accept, brings with it a multitude of new benefits. The arrival of this phase in life is inevitable, whether you want it or not, but it opens so many doors of hope and possibility.

Rather than resisting or dreading it, choose to embrace it with curiosity and excitement, and start preparing for it now. It signifies an incredible time in your life, an opportunity for personal growth and exploration, and a job well done.

My husband and I have really enjoyed dreaming big again, making a brand-new list of things we want to do together, and places we want to visit. It's been fun! Give yourself the freedom to rediscover who you are, pursue your long-awaited passions, and design your next best chapter.

With the responsibilities of raising children lessening, you'll have more time and energy to invest in your own aspirations and dreams. It's a chance to deepen connections with your partner, rekindle relationships, and embark on new adventures. While the transition to an Empty Nest might feel bittersweet, it's important to focus on the positive aspects and channel your excitement into productive endeavors.

Yes, some of it sucks. I will not deny that. But a lot of it will be amazing!

And you're not alone! Many well-known moms have talked about this chapter of life too. In an interview with Hoda Kotb,

Julia Roberts talked about becoming an Almost Empty Nester and navigating her new normal.[26] She is excited for her children to begin to forge their own path and seems like one proud mama. At the time of the interview, she still had a sixteen-year-old son at home. Looking toward her next chapter, she is excited to jump back into her career now that she has more time on her hands. After nearly two decades, Julia is in one of the most bittersweet times in her life, and she plans on making the most of it.

And Brooke Shields just recently shared a tearful video online about learning to embrace her new Empty Nest now that her youngest daughter has moved out. She said through her tears "It's not easy for the moms. We are all in this together." So true, Brooke, so true.

PREVAILING IN THE PRESENT

Now that you've taken time to look back at your motherhood journey, and before you design what your future Empty Nest years look like, let's take a look at things that are happening for you in your present, day-to-day world.

You need to understand your current reality and what your soul whispers have been trying to tell you for a long time before you make a plan for your incredible future. Let's move on to the second part of the book.

Chapter 7 Reflection Exercise

Congratulations on completing section 1. I'm so proud of you for reviewing your past with an open heart, allowing yourself time to reflect on your achievements and how far you've come, cleaning up your toolbox, and even hearing from your children. Whew, that's a lot to unpack, and if you're anything like me, this experience involved some big emotions.

Take a few minutes to reread your answers (and your children's) from the previous exercises. By having this fresh in your head, you will be better able to absorb and apply the lessons in the next section of the book.

During this phase of your life, your emotions will ebb and flow. On the more difficult days, as you reflect on your time with your kids, remember to embrace those moments when thinking about your PAST:

 Parenting is a profound journey for everyone.

 Acknowledge the beautiful moments.

 Separate yourself from your mistakes.

Trust that incredible opportunities await.

Section 2 is all about your present life, your thoughts and beliefs, identifying your current passions, and believing in yourself. Starting something fresh in midlife can be so exciting, and that's what this next section is all about.

You are doing great. Let's press on.

SECTION II

Present

CHAPTER 8

Clear the Canvas
Fresh Starts Can Feel So Good

Sunsets are proof that endings can often be beautiful too.

—BEAU TAPLIN

Becoming an Empty Nester can feel like the end of an era, but it's also a time for incredible new beginnings filled with personal growth and self-rediscovery. Now that you've taken time to reflect on your past—the work you've done, the love you've given and received, the lessons you've learned, and the amazing life you've created for your family—it's time to look at where you are today in this present moment.

Before you can plan your future, it helps to understand and assess where you are today as an individual. So much of your time has been dedicated to raising your children. Their education, sports, activities, volunteering—all the things can leave you feeling more like a chauffeur some days. But as your kids start to do things like get their driver's license, graduate, and move out, some of your time begins to open back up, and that's a good thing. You will have more freedom to pick and choose what to spend your extra time on. Empty Nesting is such a great time for making positive changes for yourself.

As you begin to go through the middle section of this book, let's pretend for a minute that you have a completely clean slate to work with. A beautiful, brand-new, empty canvas full of possibilities. A container for your soul whispers. Remember how you felt as a kid when you woke up Saturday morning looking forward to some free time? Back then, if I wasn't at swim team practice or my part-time job, you could find me watching cartoons, spending time at our local pool, collecting four leaf clovers, or playing board games with my best friend, Jill. At the young age of twelve, I had a weekday paper route, so I lived for my free, unscheduled time on the weekends. It was glorious.

Empty Nesting is a blank canvas awaiting your artistic touch.

Let's embrace that younger, carefree energy for a moment.

Empty Nesting is a blank canvas awaiting your artistic touch. It's fresh and full of possibilities. Now let's imagine for a moment that you have no limitations around time and money. Wouldn't that be nice? (I know that's unrealistic, but we are just clearing a path for your imagination. Stick with me.) This canvas has the potential to become anything you want it to be. Your own unique, personal masterpiece. I want you to think about Empty Nesting with a fresh set of eyes, ears, and an open heart, not through the lens of your limitations, but rather one of freedom and limitless possibility. You deserve to envision and believe in what is truly possible for you. This process will help ignite your imagination, uncover countless opportunities, and design the future you want. Let's expand your current level of thinking so you can make possible what might seem impossible at the moment.

GO WITH YOUR FLOW STATE

There's something special about creating from a place of pure joy and passion: Your uninhibited stream of consciousness takes over. You're in your state of *flow*. It's like tapping into an infinite well of inspiration and magic that you didn't even know existed. When you create from this place, things effortlessly start to fall into place. It's as if the universe conspires to help you in every way possible. Ideas come to you easily, and everything fits together perfectly.

This usually happens to me at about four in the morning. I wish it didn't, but it does. I often wake up and immediately start thinking about a chapter I need to work on. Ideas come to me easily in this predawn theta state of mind. Right when you awaken, your brain is fertile ground where your stream of consciousness flows effortlessly, untethered by the time constraints of the waking world. Usually, I feel like lying there, but I don't because I know I need to capture this download of information right away. I hop out of bed, go right into my kitchen where I keep my laptop, and start writing. Free of to-do lists, my mind is clear, and I'm in my state of flow.

This is the state I want you to be in when you think about your Empty Nesting possibilities. I'm not saying you need to get up at 4:00 a.m., but whenever you get those little nudges from your soul whispers, you should listen to them and jot down what comes to mind.

Author of *FLOW: Finding Love Over Worry: A Recipe for Joyful Living*, speaker, and renowned coach Kelley Wolf has been teaching this type of work for over a decade. Kelley launched her coaching practice in 2011, after graduating with a degree in clinical psychology and finishing multiple coaching certifications, most notably a master coach certification through Martha Beck. Martha is a world-renowned life coach and holds an MA and a PhD from Harvard University.

Through Kelley's amazing program, she has been able to coach people into their greatness while continuously expanding her own personal growth and knowledge from which she creates an amazing life for her beautiful family. I don't know how she does it all, so I asked her.

Kelley started her coaching career because she was fascinated by the human condition. She's committed to elevating the lives of others amidst the inevitability of human suffering. Over the years, Kelley discerned a recurring pattern: Individuals who managed to transcend their worries and fears, embracing gratitude instead, consistently reported experiencing a state she terms FLOW.

This phenomenon occurs regardless of activity or environment—be it writing, sailing, skiing, driving, surfing, walking, or socializing. The crux is not in the external circumstances but in a conscious and deliberate choice of mindset: gratitude over fear. Love over worry. Thus, FLOW emerged as a transformative, accessible tool designed to reshape mental patterns. The FLOW Method—finding (observing) love (choosing gratitude) over (despite circumstances) worry (fear and rumination)—has become a cornerstone for a life marked by joy, purpose, and gratitude. Over the years, Kelley observed that a significant segment of her clientele was Empty Nesters, although she herself was a mother to two young children and pregnant with her third.[27]

Kelley reflects,

I've been consistently intrigued by the number of clients identifying as "Empty Nesters". Many of my initial clients were women adjusting to their children going off to college, and this trend has persisted for more than a decade. Despite not being an Empty Nester myself, it seemed my teachings and methods gave great hope and peace to my amazing clients. It allowed them to access a state of joy they felt was diminishing. I was often inspired and humbled by the bravery it took to face this chapter in one's life and choose to make it as dynamic and joyful as having the children in the house.

Among Kelley's most impactful client experiences was working with a mother of twins who faced the prospect of an Empty Nest overnight. The departure of her only children, who had been the center of her life for eighteen years, was fast approaching. Through their collaboration in embracing FLOW, the client not only navigated the transition with grace but also discovered the boundless possibilities awaiting her own life's next chapter. Far from feeling "finished," she embarked on a journey to fully embrace and revel in her Empty Nest phase. She chose to see the endless opportunities that came from this transition and reported, "The chapter I most dreaded has become one of my most dynamic and interesting parts of my life."

Kelley hopes we can all be reminded of the possibilities and gifts our lives can reveal to us when we see them through a different lens.

Kelley offered this perspective, "Grieving a life stage such as children leaving the nest is critical, and then choosing to embark on the next stage with curiosity, gratitude, and love is also crucial and can be filled with unexpected joys."[28]

TRY A MINDSET SHIFT

When you think about Empty Nesting, do you feel attached to the past? Are you in a constant state of worry for your new young adult? Are you afraid you will feel lost and alone? Or are you able to remain in a state of gratitude and FLOW for their journey into adulthood and your ever-evolving nest?

I get it. Change can be hard.

But Empty Nesting is a great time to put some of that energy back into yourself and trust that your child will figure it out. When you shift your mindset from scarcity to abundance and start focusing on your dreams from that point of view, anything is possible. Choosing to embrace an abundance mindset also causes significant changes to occur in your brain.

Let's get a little "science-y" for a minute.

Psychology Today contributor, Jennice Vilhauer, PhD, states the following to be true related to positive psychology:

 Positive Neurochemistry. Thinking from a position of abundance and focusing on big dreams can stimulate the release of neurochemicals associated with positivity, such as dopamine and serotonin. These neurotransmitters create feelings of happiness, motivation, and fulfillment, which can enhance your overall well-being and drive.

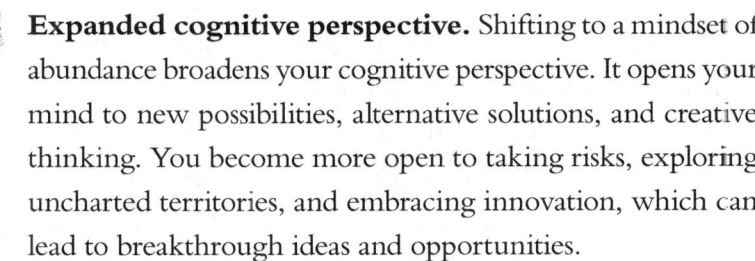

Expanded cognitive perspective. Shifting to a mindset of abundance broadens your cognitive perspective. It opens your mind to new possibilities, alternative solutions, and creative thinking. You become more open to taking risks, exploring uncharted territories, and embracing innovation, which can lead to breakthrough ideas and opportunities.

Increased resilience. Focusing on big dreams and abundance helps build resilience in your brain. You become more adaptable to setbacks and failures, seeing them as temporary obstacles rather than permanent roadblocks. This resilience enables you to bounce back quickly, learn from your experiences, and persist in pursuing your goals.

Heightened motivation. Moving toward abundant thinking fuels intrinsic motivation. When you focus on your big dreams and believe that opportunities are abundant, you experience a surge in motivation to take action, persist in the face of challenges, and continuously strive for personal growth. This increased motivation can propel you forward and drive you to achieve remarkable results as you head into your Empty Nesting years.[29]

Adopting an abundance mindset and a "clean canvas" perspective can have a transformative effect on your brain. By simply making this switch, you will significantly increase the likelihood of creating an amazing Empty Nest experience. Just by thinking and believing you can do something makes your brain work better! Fascinating. By clearing from the canvas your constraints and limiting beliefs, you will begin to see a multitude of possibilities for yourself like never before.

I promise you can bring things from your past to your new canvas, too. My hope is you'll consider the limitless possibilities ahead of you—you can put anything on that canvas you want! Trust that you will find a way to design an exciting and amazing Empty Nest experience for yourself, and as a result, you will!

Next, let's dig into what might be mentally holding you back and challenge those beliefs before you design your next best chapter.

Chapter 8 Reflection Exercise

Let's picture your blank canvas for a moment as two giant jigsaw puzzles: One has lots of pieces that represent your current commitments, while the other puzzle is blank for the moment but will soon be filled up. When you think about the first puzzle, your current life, what do you currently spend most of your waking hours doing? How many priorities (pieces) does it have? Does it stress you out or bring you peace? Rank the pieces by importance—big, medium, and small.

In this next phase of your life, some pieces will stay the same, be removed, or become larger or smaller based on their importance. This exercise allows you to visualize the amount of space that will open up for you as your children start to leave the nest and what you can do with that extra time.

Let me offer you some examples from my life. When I went from a household of five people down to three, my time freed up in so many areas. I wasn't spending as much time driving, buying food, cooking large meals, cleaning, etc. I had several extra hours back in my day because those previously big puzzle pieces shrank or completely disappeared.

Surprisingly, one of the pieces I missed the most was driving my kids around. I have spent two to three hours a day doing this for the past twenty-two years, and I bet you have too. That's crazy! I thought I wouldn't miss it, but I do. Quality time with my girls in the car was always special. It was a great time to learn about everything going on in their lives. I've now replaced that with family "FaceTimes" during our Sunday dinners. It's not as good as seeing them in person of course, but it allows our entire family to share a meal together, laugh, and catch up on what they are doing while they are away at college.

I still enjoy trying out new recipes, and I'm grateful my friends stepped up to be the taste testers! At least once a month, I make a new recipe (usually soup) and deliver it to my "soup-loving" friends. This fulfills my desire to try new recipes without worrying whether my family will eat it or not.

Yes, I know it can be sad because our babies are no longer here to take care of, but let's not go there for now. I just want you to see the possibility of prioritizing things that are important to you, fitting new things into your life that you want to do, and letting go of the ones you no longer need.

When you think about your current, completely full puzzle (and I bet it's jam-packed!), answer the following questions:

 What responsibilities take up the most space in your day?
- *Is it work, taking care of the children, activities, managing the household, working out, cooking, cleaning, etc.?*
- *Make sure to list down what the obvious big ones are, followed by the medium and small ones.*

 Which responsibilities will decrease as your children start to move out?

 What puzzle pieces are going to fall off that you really enjoy doing?

How can you add something similar back in to replace it?

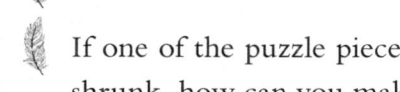 If one of the puzzle pieces you personally love to do has shrunk, how can you make it bigger?

Taking time to focus on what you love about your life right now and what's about to change is important.

 When you look at your puzzle pieces all together, does it create a beautiful picture of the life you want?

 How can you adjust your priorities to add more joy into your life?

 Which pieces are most important to you as you head into your Empty Nesting years?

 Which pieces do you need to take out completely?

You've poured a lot of love into creating this beautiful life of yours. I want to make sure you add the things you love to do into your new puzzle, which is your blank canvas for your Empty Nest life.

This is an important part of the book because your future can look any way you want it to. It really can! Make sure you take time to fit in all the beautiful puzzle pieces you want to carry into this next phase of life. This puzzle represents your midlife masterpiece.

I hope all your wishes and dreams make it onto your new, blank canvas. Let's take a quick look at what you believe is possible for your Empty Nesting years and make sure you are dreaming big enough before you create your Empty Nest Game Plan.

Thoughts and Beliefs
Declutter Your Mind to Harness the Power Within

Your thoughts and beliefs shape your reality,
for when you change your mind,
you change your life.

—DR. JOE DISPENZA

It's been said that we are what we think, and there's a lot of truth to that. Our thoughts, beliefs, and actions all play a role in shaping our reality. If we want to create a positive reality for ourselves, we need to focus on creating a powerful mindset to support that. Having an abundance mindset focused on limitless possibilities is crucial before you step into this next phase of life.

Let's dig into some neuroscience that supports these facts.

In 2017, I attended my first Dr. Joe Dispenza event, and to say it was life-changing would be an understatement. Dr.

Joe Dispenza is a *New York Times* best-selling author, speaker, and researcher best known for his work on the intersection of neuroscience, quantum physics, and the power of the mind. He holds a PhD in neuroscience and is renowned for his teachings on the potential of the human mind to rewire itself and create positive change in one's life through techniques such as meditation, visualization, and mindfulness.

Back then I knew his programs would help me on my mental health and cancer journey, so I finally decided to go. It was incredible. The concepts and meditations I learned over the course of those two weeks have changed me forever. I still practice his teachings today. It made me realize how powerful our thoughts, beliefs, feelings, and actions truly are, and how they have a huge impact on our body, mind, and soul.

Break free from unconscious patterns and create positive change in your life.

In his New York Times bestseller, *Breaking the Habit of Being Yourself,* Dr. Joe also explores the concept of neuroplasticity.[30] He emphasizes that your thoughts and beliefs are not just fleeting mental events but have a tangible impact on your biology and overall well-being.

He argues that by becoming aware of your thoughts and beliefs, you can begin to break free from unconscious patterns and create positive change in your life. It's so important to clear from your canvas these outdated, unconscious patterns of thinking. This will allow you to bring new, exciting, and fulfilling experiences into your life. Dr. Joe says, "We've in fact conditioned ourselves to believe all sorts of things that aren't necessarily true—and many of these things are having a negative impact on our health and happiness."[31]

THE POWER OF CHANGING YOUR MIND

According to Dr. Joe, when you constantly think and feel in certain ways, you develop a familiar personality and create a reality that aligns with that personality. However, by consciously choosing new thoughts and beliefs, you can transform your personality and, consequently, your reality. He emphasizes the importance of rewiring your brain through focused intention, meditation, and visualization. By envisioning your desired outcomes and embodying the emotions associated with those outcomes, you can reprogram your neural networks and create a new reality.[32]

In essence, Dr. Joe Dispenza's work highlights the profound influence your thoughts and beliefs have on your life, and offers practical techniques to harness this power for positive transformation. He encourages individuals to break free from limiting patterns, embrace new possibilities, and consciously create lives they desire through intentional thoughts and beliefs.

Are your current thoughts around Empty Nesting skewed toward the positive and full of possibility? Or more toward the negative, filled with fear of the unknown and your changing identity?

My thoughts leaned slightly toward the latter until I started thinking about Empty Nesting in a more intentional and empowered way. After spending the past several years researching this topic, I discovered there is a huge disconnect between what people believe happens during Empty Nesting and what is actually possible.

Never before in history have we had access to this many resources to help create a fulfilling second act—to define our next best chapter. If you want to write a compelling article, book, or song, you can take a MasterClass from your favorite writer. If you want to get better at a certain language, there's an app for that. And if you want to get better at juggling, well, there are YouTube videos for that, too. Everyone has access to turn unique dreams into realities, so why aren't more people doing it?

It's complicated.

During an interview with Dirk Nevelle, founder of the *Finding Your Genius Zone* podcast, we covered this very important topic.[33] We discussed how some of us learned at an early age to play it safe and believed it was impossible to achieve our dream goal or find our dream job. We both discovered we were still carrying those beliefs around with us today. Whether it resulted from low self-esteem, bullying, or lack of faith, this feeling had been with us our entire lives. We are now just beginning to do the work to change our internal conversations. During the interview, Dirk said something really profound that stuck with me.

We were discussing fear of failure and what that meant to us. We agreed that failing at something you absolutely love and have always wanted to do has very different emotions attached to it than failing at something that's maybe just a job or not that important to you. We both picked careers we were very good at, but they weren't aligned with our true calling.

He said, "It can be a very exhausting life running a race you really don't want to win."

And it hit me like a ton of bricks. Why do people put so much blood, sweat, and tears into things that they are good at but don't light them up from within? Why do you sometimes feel like you have no choice in life but to accept life as it is? To stay in the same job, situation, or relationship when it no longer serves you?

I understand everyone needs to put food on the table, but what if you could do that while simultaneously fulfilling your most sacred desires? Your true passion? When he said that, I could no longer run from what I had been doing for decades. I had been ignoring a few of my soul whispers and knew I had to change.

After that podcast, I got up earlier to work on my book, kicked my inner critics to the curb and instead, trusted my inner compass. I stopped caring what other people thought about me and began to check in with myself more often. I now surround myself with people who share my vision for life and encourage me rather than put me down and dismiss me. I've even started singing again, and it feels so good.

DREAMERS CAN BECOME DOERS

What if you put as much time and energy into your dreams as you possibly could, instead of just thinking about them? I believe it would change the world for the better on so many levels. There are so many inspiring examples of people who struggled with self-doubt but kept on their path once they chose it and went on to change the world. They had a burning desire to see it through, despite the naysayers.

One famous figure who struggled with this but still achieved extraordinary success is the renowned physicist Albert Einstein. In his early years, he faced numerous challenges and setbacks, struggled with formal education, and could not find employment as a young physicist. I had no idea! Despite his exceptional intelligence and creativity, he encountered resistance from the academic and scientific communities due to his unorthodox ideas and unconventional approach to physics.

Einstein's path to recognition was marked by self-doubt and frustration. His groundbreaking theories, including the theory of relativity, were initially met with skepticism and resistance. He faced rejection and criticism from established scholars, and his work was often misunderstood.[34] However, Einstein persisted in pursuing his passions and refining his theories, gradually overcoming the limiting beliefs that had held him back.

Through perseverance and a steadfast commitment to his ideas, he eventually gained recognition for his revolutionary contributions to the field of physics. Where would we be today without his self-belief, commitment, and persistence? He changed our world forever.

If Einstein can overcome his self-doubt, so can you. Challenge yourself to stop defending your limiting beliefs and letting them hold you back. They aren't doing you any good. When I start to have a limiting belief creep up, I like to play this little game with myself called FLIP it! I FLIP any thought that doesn't serve me into the positive opposite. FLIP stands for Feel Like It's Possible. I love a good acronym. It's so simple, but it works so well.

When I started writing this book, for example, I thought, "No one would read it. I'm an unknown author. How will my audience ever find me? How can I find a great publisher? I want to help women rediscover who they are before their kids leave the nest. What if this doesn't work the way I hope it will?"

Then I would instantly FLIP those thoughts and think, "What if this book does find the right audience, helps a lot of women, and they begin to organically share it with their friends who need it too? What if book clubs form around the country, and the conversation around Empty Nesting becomes elevated to a level of joy, purpose, and contentment?" That's what I want to manifest. P.S. I would love to drop in on some of those book clubs virtually! That would be amazing.

When you find yourself stuck with a recurring limiting belief, try this exercise and FLIP it. Because I promise you, it can change your perspective in an instant and open a doorway you could not see before.

So what exactly *do* you want to do in your Empty Nesting years?

Now that you have had a moment to think about what is possible for your future, what is it exactly? How would your life look in the near future if you took time to intentionally create it? Sometimes people know exactly what they want to do, and that's great. However, more often than not, people need prompts to dive into and discover what they were naturally born to do. Let's press on . . .

Chapter 9 Reflection Exercise

By diving deep into any limiting beliefs you have, you will gain valuable insight into the stories you tell yourself and the impact they have on your life. Recognizing the duration of these thoughts, where they came from, and their relevance in your present reality empowers you to separate yourself from the burden of your outdated narratives.

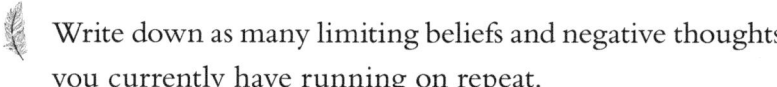

- Write down as many limiting beliefs and negative thoughts you currently have running on repeat.

- How long have you had these thoughts?

- When did they start, and why?

- Are these true for you today, or are they old stories?

- Did they start with you or someone else? Take the time to explain their origins if you can remember them.

- What have these limitations stood in the way of you achieving?

- What are you willing to do about it today?

It's okay if a lot comes up. You've been alive for many years, my friend. But let's make sure these limiting beliefs don't follow you into your Empty Nest.

Now take a minute and FLIP each of your negative beliefs into a more positive narrative. Write down the opposite for every limiting belief you have.

Clearing away these limitations opens up new possibilities and paves the way for your personal growth.

Heading into this next chapter of your life with these cobwebs cleared out will allow you to create your new passion project from a clearer point of view. How refreshing is that?!

The Ten Cs
The Path to Your Purpose

The only way to do great work is to love what you do. If you haven't found it yet, keep looking, and don't settle. As with all matters of the heart, you'll know when you find it.

—STEVE JOBS

Several years ago, I started to notice how much unscheduled time I had during the day. When two of my daughters were still in high school and had after-school theater activities, I spent up to ten hours a day by myself. I was working a very lenient part-time job back then, so that still left me with many hours in the day feeling alone and wanting to find something fulfilling to do with my extra time.

When I started exploring what to do with my extra time, so many options opened up to me. I was overwhelmed, couldn't focus, and ended up wasting a lot of time doing nothing. I felt like I was keeping myself busy with little projects here and there, but they didn't last for long. This is a common phenomenon, and it is called decision fatigue.

Does that ever happen to you? It's frustrating, right? I used to suffer from it extensively. My ADHD brain had me starting and stopping projects for years. I found myself enamored with several great ideas and possibilities, but didn't follow through on a lot of them.

If this is happening to you, let's change that right here, right now. When I was going through this, to help me gain more clarity about what I wanted for my life, I started with these four basic questions:

- What have I always wanted to do?

- Who have I always wanted to be?

- What have I always wanted to learn?

- Who have I always wanted to help?

My answers were as follows. I want to . . .

- Write a book to create more impact, community, and connection in our world.

- Be a better writer and singer.

- Learn how to rediscover my unique passions and help others do the same.

- Help moms break the cycle of playing small and putting themselves last.

This was a good start, but I quickly expanded my list of questions to understand what was truly important to me on a soul level. When you ask deeper questions, you get better answers. This is what I came up with. It worked for me, and I hope it does for you too.

I'm going to take you through a self-discovery exercise called the Ten Cs. It's the heart and foundation of this book. These questions will guide you to choose your next best thing. When I took myself through this more in-depth exercise, it

> *When you ask deeper questions, you get better answers.*

stripped away my fear, self-doubt, and uncertainty. I clearly understand what is (and is not) important to me, and now I believe my dreams are very possible. You are going to learn more about your unique and incredible soul whispers.

The Ten Cs are ten words to reflect on to help you discover your current passions and interests. Don't worry, you don't have to make a really long list. But do write down a few thoughts for each word as they come to mind:

 CONNECTION

What are you deeply *connected* to in your life? This could be a person/place/thing.

 CONVERSATION

What do you find yourself always *conversing* about? You can talk about this for hours.

 CHALLENGING

What *challenges* do you enjoy? Or have you overcome something where sharing your story might benefit others?

COMPASSION

What brings out your *compassion*? What pulls at your heartstrings?

CONTRIBUTION

How do you like to *contribute* to those around you? In what ways do you like to make a difference?

CONVICTION

What are you *convicted* about? What is at the core of your belief system?

CURIOSITY

What are you *curious* about? What has always piqued your interest?

CREATIVITY

What kind of *creative* outlets do you enjoy? What is something new you want to learn?

COMMUNITY

What does *community* mean to you? How do you like to make an impact?

CELEBRATION

What do you love to *celebrate* about life? What brings you joy?

Writing down answers to these ten questions will get you closer to your purpose, I promise. Take a good amount of time on these, and focus on what matters to you on a soul level. Has it been a while since you've thought about these things? I get it! I was right there with you.

Take another glance at your list. Do any themes appear? Any repeat answers? Does one stand out as the clear winner? Sit with your list and see which answers resonate with you the most. And please don't stress about picking the right one. We'll get to that next. Just see which ones bubble up to the top. Let me share a personal example that might help you with this process.

In 2019, I was asked to co-host a TV show with my dear friend, Terry Sidford, at Park City Television. We have a small station here in town, and we were grateful the owner gave us the opportunity. Terry and I both share a passion for helping people get their stories out into the world, so it felt like a good fit. We had a ton of fun working together and were on air for about a year interviewing incredibly diverse and impactful locals about their passion projects.

Unfortunately, the station downsized, and our show was canceled. Luckily, through one of my interviews, I met a Main Street venue owner and started helping him promote their new music shows. My favorite one was all about Nashville songwriters. I love country music, so I had hit the jackpot! This new opportunity addressed seven of my Ten Cs:

 Music—my creativity, and I converse about it all the time

 Bringing together my community—connection and community

 Showcasing talented songwriters—compassion and conviction

Seeing how impactful these events were to our attendees—contentment

Promoting these shows then led me to work on the very first Park City Songwriter Festival. It was magical. However, after six short months, COVID-19 shut everything down. Two years later, when the pandemic started to lift, the festival director and I decided to bring a few of these incredible songwriter experiences to my hometown in Washington and my cul-de-sac here in Park City for friends and neighbors to enjoy. It was just what the world needed, and they are still going on today.

Just pick what's nudging you the most and get started.

There's a great lesson in this story. I started with the TV opportunity, which was fun, and then it led me to two of my true loves in life—music and community. I could have seen our TV station downsizing as a failure, but it wasn't at all! It led me to my next best thing.

So don't worry. Just pick what's nudging you the most and get started. I promise you will be rewarded for taking action, and it will ping-pong you toward your purpose.

IT'S NOT TOO LATE

How to choose? What to pick? If your purpose made its way to the top of the list, great. If not, and you're unsure of what to focus on, that's okay. If you're like most people, you probably have several ideas about what your next chapter might look like, but you're not sure where to start. And believing you can create an amazing second act might feel impossible. But that's just your own Itty-Bitty Shitty Committee talking smack to you. As you learn to tune those voices out and tune back into yourself, you will realize you have plenty of time to create something new for yourself. New experiences. New joy. New success.

There are so many stories about well-known people who went through this same journey. Morgan Freeman, one of my favorite actors, wasn't taken seriously until his fifties, even though he had been acting for decades. Now he's one of the best of the best. Julia Child didn't publish her famous book *Mastering the Art of French Cooking* until she was forty-nine. And Susan Boyle, the Scottish singer who rose to international fame in 2009 through her appearance on the reality show *Britain's Got Talent,* was forty-seven when she got her turn in the spotlight.

These individuals demonstrate that no matter how ginormous your dream is, age doesn't have to be a barrier to success. Ryan Tedder said in a recent interview that there is no longer ageism in music.[35] That's been *unheard of* up until now.

> *It's time to begin your journey and develop your next best thing.*

Huge news! It opens up amazing possibilities for everyone no matter what your age.

Let's take a look at your Ten Cs results and see if there is a clear winner, or at least a great starting point. It's time to begin your journey and develop your next best thing.

Chapter 10 Reflection Exercise

After you answered the Ten Cs questions, are you surprised by any of your answers that bubbled up? What themes do you see? Were old dreams making their way to the surface? Which ones resonate with you the most?

For now, go back to your list, and circle your top five that repeatedly made the list. It doesn't mean you won't get to the others, but we want to see which five are rising to the top. If you have a clear number one, circle it and move on to the next chapter. That's great. If you have five, that's great too. Next, think about the five things you circled and how they would impact the following areas of your life:

- Your personal happiness and health

- Your marriage or partnership

- Your children

- Friends and family

- A new audience that may need your service or story

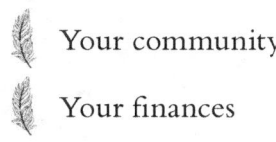 Your community

Your finances

When I made my list, my top five were singing, songwriting, learning guitar, writing a book, and starting a business. However, when I went through the second part of this exercise, it was so clear to me that it was my time to write a book. I was in the best position to serve my audience at this point in my life because I was living exactly what I wanted to write about and help other mothers through.

It's the best decision I ever made because it allowed me to feel fulfilled while knowing I was creating something to impact the world in a positive way. Choosing to work on a book helped me get back in the habit of working on a project with meaning, and it gave me a newfound purpose which my family got to witness.

It's a good use of your time every few months or so to check back in with yourself and revisit your Ten Cs. That way, you can see whether you are on track putting time into what you love in your day-to-day life, or if you have gotten off course and need to change direction.

Your priorities will continue to evolve and shift over time. And by staying in tune with that, you can make sure you're focusing on the things that matter most to you.

Your One Thing
What Lights You Up?

Whatever you do, or dream you can do, begin it.
Boldness has genius, power, and magic in it.

—JOHANN WOLFGANG VON GOETHE

You made a list of what you are really passionate about, but how do you decide where to start? Are you worried about picking the wrong thing? Don't be. In this chapter, we discuss the power of taking intentional action. There really isn't a wrong choice. Starting with one goal and following that clue can ultimately lead you to your intended destination. It puts stagnant energy in motion and can create a ripple effect in every area of your life.

It might feel overwhelming and stressful to narrow your choices down to one. For example, if you choose this, then you won't have that. If you do this, you will miss out on that. I get it. FOMO is real. But believe it or not, making the decision isn't actually the hard part. It's the expectations you tie to your decision that paralyze you. Instead, assess and adjust your expectations to clear a path to your best jumping-in point.

The word *decide* comes from the Latin roots *de*, which means "of or from," and *cide*, which means "to cut or cut off from."[36] This implies that making a decision involves cutting off other options and possibilities. But that's not the case here. You are just picking your One Thing to work on for now and delaying your work on the others. This will allow you to focus on your one true passion and not get spread too thin by trying to do it all.

Take some time to define what "your best" means to you.

But here's where you could get into trouble. Once you pick something new to work on, or if you're dusting off an old project, oftentimes you start to put an enormous amount of pressure on yourself to be *the best*. When really, the only responsibility you have is to learn your craft and do *your best*. Those are two very different things. Take some time to define what "your best" means to you. This will ease the stress of picking your One Thing and allow you to enjoy the process more thoroughly. When you can view your choice through the lens of "what does a successful outcome look like to *me*," making a decision becomes much easier. Get comfortable with your One Thing, and trust where it will lead you.

FOCUS TO REMOVE YOUR FREEZE RESPONSE

As I mentioned earlier, I wasted so much time wanting to learn too many things, got overwhelmed, and ended up not doing much at all. I could have been much farther down the road if I had just stuck with my One Thing, worked on that, and waited to see where that led me next. When has this happened to you?

I think it's easy to do because we lead busy lives, and believe we have all the time in the world to work on our dreams in the future. We don't. It's time to seize the day now. When your kids start moving out, it's time to focus and take intentional action. It's best to start with one area of life, your One Thing. Here's a little science behind this fact.

The reason humans can only effectively focus on one thing at a time is due to the inherent limitations of their cognitive processing capabilities.[37] (Oh good, so scientists are saying it's not our fault. Whew!) The human brain has a finite capacity for attention and cannot fully engage in multiple tasks simultaneously without experiencing a significant decline in performance.

When individuals attempt to divide their attention across multiple activities, their cognitive resources become stretched thin, leading to reduced concentration, impaired decision-making, and decreased overall productivity.[38] This phenomenon, known as "attentional bottleneck," arises from the brain's limited capacity to process and filter information.[39] By focusing on a single task, humans can allocate their cognitive resources more efficiently, allowing for deeper engagement, improved information processing, and enhanced task performance. Working on one thing at a time is easier, and it makes our brains happier.

When I began to focus my attention back on my dreams and desires, I wanted to do it all, and I bet you do too! I felt a new spark of energy and inspiration I hadn't felt in years. Suddenly, so many things became possible, whereas in the past, I had believed those possibilities were out of reach. I'm glad that this time around, I chose to work on my One Thing instead of spreading myself too thin. I stuck with it, stayed focused, and went really deep on the topic. It works. Think about this for a moment. What if everyone in the world started working on something they were deeply passionate about—their One Thing? It would change our world forever.

Viola Davis, the acclaimed American actress known for her powerful performances onstage and onscreen, exemplifies the impact of focus and dedication in the world of acting. With a background in theater and a deep passion for acting, she immersed herself in the art of performance, studying her craft and honing her skills through extensive training

Your One Thing can positively impact several areas of your life.

and experience. Because of her unwavering commitment to portraying complex and multifaceted characters, Viola Davis has garnered critical acclaim and numerous awards, including an Academy Award, an Emmy Award, and multiple Tony Awards.[40] Her journey from being an aspiring actor to a celebrated star underscores the transformative power of focus, passion, and perseverance in achieving success in the competitive world of acting. Her work is truly inspiring.

I know it might seem hard, but for now I would like you to pick One Thing from your list of five that you want to work on. Trust yourself and stick with the choice that is naturally bubbling up to the top. And like a domino, this has the potential to put into motion so many other goals you want to achieve. We can only effectively focus on one thing at a time, but your One Thing can positively impact several areas of your life and others around you.

THERE'S NO TIME LIKE
THE PRESENT

Let's pick your One Thing right now. Don't overthink it, just do it. Go with your gut. Close your eyes, and say out loud the very first one that comes to mind. Write it down, and sit with it for a few minutes. You can always come back and change it later, but for now let's assume this is your number one choice. Would spending time on this make you extremely happy? Then that is the one you should pick. Time is your most valuable currency, so plan to use it well.

When I chose to write a book, I was nervous at first. I thought I might miss out on other opportunities, but when I looked back at my Ten Cs list, I realized a book would do so much more for my dreams than just become a book. It would

- make my *connection* with friends stronger

- create a new *community* with parents at a similar stage in life

- *challenge* me to learn new things

- allow my *creativity* to shine

- give me something new to *converse* about

- be a great *contribution* to society and

- give me new *conviction* and something to *celebrate*

Writing a book checked off almost every Ten Cs box for me. When you think about your One Thing, do you see how it can have a ripple effect in your life? You've taken the plunge and picked a new hobby, goal, or passion project to focus on. Congratulations! It's always exciting to embark on a new adventure.

Once you've made the decision to start, however, there's something you need to be aware of. Guess who's going to kick into high gear right about now? Yep. You guessed it. Your inner critic can be relentless trying to talk you out of what you are about to start.

Choosing to do something new unleashes fears, doubts, and disbeliefs that are buried deep within your subconscious, and your inner critic may try to convince you to quit too soon before the magic happens. We need to talk about the science behind why this happens so you aren't derailed right out of the gate. In the next chapter, we'll give your inner critic a one-two punch and a left hook out of nowhere.

Chapter 11 Reflection Exercise

Focusing on your One Thing can initiate a cascade of transformative benefits that will positively impact many aspects of your life. Write down the ways you envision your life changing for the better if you stick with your One Thing and really give it your best shot.

 What new disciplines will you develop?

 How will it feel to cultivate determination and grit in the pursuit of this endeavor?

 Who in your life will be affected in a positive way seeing you work on your passion project?

 How could it have a domino effect in your life?

 How will you feel when you wake up in the morning?

 What are some new things you can talk about with friends and family?

 By working on your One Thing, how do you see it leading you to eventually work on your other soul whispers?

The act of picking your One Thing and cultivating it creates a powerful effect, ushering in a renewed sense of purpose, self-discovery, and personal growth. It's the perfect place to be when you start planning for what you want in your Empty Nesting years. Nice job!

Inner Critic vs. Inner Compass

Busting through the BS to Discover Your True North

*I deeply believe that each one of us has an inner compass
that points us towards our true north, and if we have
the courage to listen and follow it, we can navigate our
way to a life of authenticity, purpose, and joy.*

—GLENNON DOYLE

I'm glad you picked your One Thing to focus on, and I
look forward to seeing where it takes you. This is a very
important first step. Consistently taking baby steps forward is
when the magic starts to happen. Sometimes when we finally
have the courage to start something new, we begin with so much
enthusiasm and quit a few weeks later. We beat ourselves up for
repeating this pattern year after year. And so the cycle ensues.

The diet industry is a perfect example of this. It thrives on our
predictable self-sabotaging behaviors and makes billions of dollars

off us annually. If society better understood why this happens and how we could disrupt our habitual behaviors, we would be so much more empowered as a collective. Let's break down the science behind why the inner critic pops up right when we finally start something new and how to overcome this when it happens.

When you decide to make a change, various processes within your brain get triggered. The prefrontal cortex, responsible for decision-making and goal-setting gets activated, initiating a conscious intention to change. The limbic system (which governs emotions and engages fear) tunes in as well, since change often involves stepping out of your comfort zone and facing uncertainty.[41] It is during this transformative phase that the inner critic tends to emerge.

The inner critic represents a collection of thoughts and beliefs that are deeply ingrained within you, originating from your past experiences and external influences.[42] Its role is to protect you from potential threats and maintain the status quo by discouraging change. The inner critic manifests itself as self-doubt, negative self-talk, and fear of failure, attempting to dissuade you from taking risks or deviating from familiar patterns. This is why when you start something new—for example, a workout routine or way of eating—you can do it for a while but eventually run out of steam and feel defeated. Understanding these concepts helps you give yourself some grace for what you've been doing for so long. It's not that you don't value follow-through or have willpower. It's your brain.

MAKING THE SHIFT

The inner critic is in the part of your brain responsible for anxiety as well.[43] It will fire off thoughts and signals to get you to go back to your old ways in order to remain calm. It feels threatened when we do something new, and the brain strongly prefers the familiar. Recognizing the role of the inner critic is essential so we can finally break free from this frustrating cycle.

However, the goal isn't to turn off your inner critic entirely because there is a lot you can learn from it. For example, when I was trying out for *X Factor*, my inner critic was on fire. It was relentless. All that internal chatter was proof that I was about to go do something really important to me. I pushed through it, quieted down those self-defeating thoughts throughout the day, and completed my audition.

The ultimate goal is to turn down the inner critic's volume, take back control, and put you back in the driver's seat. You were never designed to be led by your brain. The brain was designed to be your servant, not your master. You were meant to lead with your heart and trust your gut. That's why the gut is called the second brain. Trust your gut, always.

How does your inner critic like to show up? What does it say to you? What weapon or weakness does it use against you to stop believing in yourself? And why do you listen to it when you know it's not speaking the truth? Instead of focusing so much on the inner critic, it's time to tune into your true north—your inner compass. Let's discuss how to do that.

You were meant to lead with your heart and trust your gut.

From day one, you have carried with you an inner compass, an internal knowing. It's always guiding you even when you aren't listening. It is the life force that has shaped your decisions, values, and aspirations. It's the unwavering voice within you that whispers to you continuously, reminding you of your purpose and who you are authentically. Now more than ever, as you navigate this stage of life, it is crucial to reconnect with your inner compass.

Your inner compass possesses a remarkable ability to recognize signs of synchronicity—those serendipitous moments that seem to be laced with cosmic intention. It is in these instances that you can reaffirm your connection to your true north, your inherent self. Just as each cup of tea is uniquely steeped to match your individual tastes and preferences, so too is your journey through life tailored specifically to you, as if orchestrated by the universe itself. Embracing these subtle yet profound encounters, the quiet whispers of your destiny, puts you on a path that will lead you to your purpose. They allow your story to unfold with grace and ease.

Ideally, as an Almost Empty Nester, your inner compass will become a trusted adviser. Your new favorite road trip companion guiding you through uncharted territory. Your inner critic has no business being in your brand-new toolbox. Turn that volume way down, and don't believe what it says to you for one minute. Listen to your inner compass. Always.

Your Inner Compass possesses a remarkable ability to recognize signs of synchronicity.

Rekindle your relationship with this guiding force, and find the courage to trust its wisdom. Continue on your new path with confidence. As you embark on your journey, you will encounter challenges, doubts, and uncertainties for sure. Choose to listen to your inner compass and embrace its guidance. It will navigate you toward a life rooted in fulfillment and authenticity. You have much better odds of achieving your One Thing when you are aligned with your inner compass.

FOLLOWING HER COMPASS

Sara Blakely is a great example of someone who ignored her inner critic and relentlessly pursued her dream to make women feel better in their clothing. She wanted to revolutionize women's undergarments with her innovative shapewear concept, SPANX. However, when she started out, she faced numerous challenges and doubts from her inner critic. As a young woman selling fax machines door-to-door, Sara struggled with self-doubt and the fear of failure. Despite these obstacles, she believed in her idea and refused to let her inner critic hold her back.

With just $5,000 in savings and a strong vision, Sara launched SPANX from her apartment. She faced rejection from multiple manufacturers and investors, but she persisted, learning from her setbacks and refining her product. Sara's breakthrough came when Oprah Winfrey endorsed SPANX, leading to a surge in demand and catapulting the brand to success. Despite her initial doubts and fears, Sara's perseverance and belief in herself paid off, and SPANX became a household name known for empowering women and reshaping the fashion industry.[44]

Her story is a testament to the power of resilience, self-confidence, and determination in the face of adversity. By challenging her inner critic, she turned her dream into a reality and built a billion-dollar business that continues to help women around the world feel confident and comfortable in their own skin. Hallelujah! Thank God, she didn't quit. I wear my SPANX all the time.

In some cases, your inner critic has been there a really long time, and it's hard to ignore the things it's telling you. I get it. It's a challenge. I invite you to instead get out of your head and see the possibilities you have through the lens of a friend. Friends can often see a clearer path to our purpose that we cannot, and can give us much-needed encouragement and positive perspective. Let's hear what they have to say, right after your next reflection exercise.

Chapter 12 Reflection Exercise

Haven't listened to your inner compass in a while? Been listening to your inner critic too much? I hear you.

Oftentimes you need to get outside of yourself to see what's possible. You need to squash those scarcity glasses today and adjust the lens with which you see the world to embrace your own uniqueness, unlimited potential, and incredible possibilities. You are the only one who can choose to leave the inner critic's opinions behind and instead listen to the voice of your inner compass that keeps you on the right path forward.

Let's do that now. Grab your journal, and draw a line down the middle of the page. On the left side, make a list of what your inner critic is saying about your new goals. On the right side, list everything your inner compass is saying. Notice the major differences in the tone of voice. Who would you rather listen to?

There's a Native American story that ties perfectly to this analogy. It talks about how you have two wolves residing within you, one representing positive qualities and the other representing negative.[45] The essence of the tale lies in the recognition that the wolf who prevails is the one you choose to feed.

By consciously nourishing the virtues and values that align with your highest self, you will cultivate a positive mindset and develop more confidence. It's time to starve your inner critic and feed your inner compass.

It's a simple success strategy, and it is crucial during this time of your life. This is such a beautiful way to live, and it will rub off on your children in a positive way, too. When they observe you using more confident self-talk language, quieting your fears and doubts, and encouraging yourself more, they will start to do the same.

Lens of a Friend

Outside Perspective Can Be so Beautiful

Sometimes it takes the perspective of a friend to unveil the hidden possibilities within ourselves.

—UNKNOWN

One of the best ways to quickly bust through the BS of your inner critic is through the lens of a trusted friend. They see you—not through your personal, self-imposed filter of fear and doubt, but through the lens of possibility and unwavering belief in your gifts. Their powerful insights have the potential to cut through your internal noise and dismantle the invisible barriers you have constructed for yourself.

Your bestie sees your gifts. They see your soul. They can easily remind you of your unique talents, strengths, and limitless potential. Seeing your next chapter in life through this lens strengthens your spirit of adventure and fosters a greater belief in yourself. You will move forward with more confidence as you embark on your transformative journey.

Without this outside perspective and left to your own devices, you may find yourself all too swiftly focusing on the possible downsides of your own goals and dreams, even as you easily spot the potential in others. This can be attributed to a cognitive bias known as self-negativity bias.[46] And you know by now I do love me some good science. This bias stems from various psychological factors, including self-doubt, fear of failure, and a tendency to focus on past negative experiences. When it comes to ourselves, we tend to be more critical, cautious, and self-protective, which limits our perspective and narrows our perception of what's possible.

Supporting yourself as you would a dear friend empowers you to embrace a more positive and expansive vision for your life.

However, when we shift our perspective and adopt the mindset of a supportive friend, our cognitive lens changes instantly. By altering your viewpoint, it will allow you to distance yourself from self-judgment and tap into a more compassionate and optimistic mindset. Treating your own goals and aspirations (and your One Thing) as if they were those of a loved one will help you explore a wider range of options, challenge your self-limiting beliefs, and unlock a clear path to success. Supporting yourself as you would a dear friend empowers you to embrace a more positive and expansive vision for your life.

A SUPPORT SYSTEM SUCCESS STORY

One of my favorite real-life stories about someone who initially lacked self-belief but went on to achieve unimaginable success with the support of others is J. K. Rowling, the renowned author of the *Harry Potter* series. In interviews, she continuously thanks her friends and family for not giving up on her because she was so close to giving up on her dream. Before the *Harry Potter* books took the world by storm, J. K. Rowling faced numerous personal and professional challenges. She was a single mother living on welfare and struggling with depression. Rowling had a deep passion for writing and had been working on a manuscript for a fantasy novel, but she faced painful rejections from multiple publishers who did not see the potential in her work.

During this challenging period, Rowling found solace and encouragement from her friends and family. In particular, it was her best friend, Sean Harris, who played a significant role in her journey to success. He saw the brilliance in her storytelling and repeatedly urged her not to give up. With her best friend's support, Rowling persevered and continued to refine her manuscript. Finally, Bloomsbury, a publishing company in the United Kingdom, took a chance on her book *Harry Potter and the Philosopher's Stone* (known as *Harry Potter and the Sorcerer's Stone* in the United States). The book was met with critical acclaim and quickly gained popularity among young readers.

The success of the first *Harry Potter* book marked the beginning of a literary phenomenon. Rowling went on to publish six more books in the series, each one receiving immense praise and amassing a global fanbase. The Harry Potter franchise expanded to include movies, merchandise, theme parks, and more, turning J. K. Rowling into one of the most well-known and influential authors in the world.[47] Amazing!

J. K. Rowling's story demonstrates the transformative power of encouragement, support from loved ones, and not giving up on your dreams. Despite her initial self-doubt and the obstacles she faced, the support and motivation she received from her friends and family propelled her forward. She was given the gift of seeing her writing through the lens of her best friend, and that kept her going. This enabled her to create a beloved literary universe that continues to inspire and captivate millions of readers worldwide.

YOUR BIGGEST CHEERLEADER—YOURSELF

If you look back on your One Thing, do you have any self-doubt surrounding it? How would your best friend respond to you if you told him or her about your One Thing? What if your best friend came to you with their One Thing, their biggest dream? Wouldn't you immediately see all the exciting and incredible possibilities for them? You would probably instantly see their path to success. It's so much easier to encourage someone else, but not as easy when it comes to yourself. Let's commit to changing that right now. Commit to treating *yourself* as one of your very best friends for the rest of your life.

Commit to treating yourself as one of your very best friends for the rest of your life.

Your ideas matter as much as your best friend's, so make sure to wear your new glasses throughout the rest of this journey.

See your future possibilities through this lens, rather than your inner critic's lens. Throw those in the garbage where they belong. Forever.

You have a duty to take care of yourself and your inner child for the rest of your life. Encourage her. Support her. Believe in her. Nurture her. Have fun. Just because you look all grown up on the outside doesn't mean you still don't have the dreams of your younger self on the inside. And those dreams deserve your love and attention. Right now. It's time to make room for more playtime.

As you start to pursue a new passion project and creative endeavor, it may come as a surprise that not all of your closest friends will enthusiastically support your journey. This phenomenon is a common theme many authors and creators encounter. While most friends will cheer you on and stand by your side every step of the way, some may not show the same level of interest or support that you had hoped for. That's okay. Do it anyway. It's important to remember that everyone has their own preferences, priorities, and limitations.

Your passion project is a reflection of your unique vision and creativity, and those who truly appreciate and resonate with your work will find their way to it. Embrace the support you receive, no matter where it comes from, be grateful, and continue to pursue your dreams with determination and resilience.

Chapter 13 Reflection Exercise

Take a moment and embody the energy you possess when your best friend comes to you with a great idea. You don't see limitations for them because it's not you you're thinking about. Right? Or if you do see some minor roadblocks, you usually can see a path around them.

For this exercise, we're going to embody the energy of looking at your One Thing from the outside in. That's how you want to approach this—through the lens of your loving best friend.

Whoever is your biggest champion in life, I want you to embody that voice right now. That energy. That love. It took a lot of courage for you to pick your One Thing, so let's give you some encouragement and positive feedback from that outside lens. Put your "bestie" glasses on, and answer these questions:

 Why does your idea seem like a great one?

 How will it fulfill you on a soul level?

What possibilities do you envision for how this might actually work out?

What does success look like for you?

How can you encourage yourself to take the first action step despite not seeing the finish line?

When was the last time you did something for yourself just for the joy of it?

How will it feel waking up in the morning knowing you are going to spend your time doing something you love?

Who in the world would greatly benefit from you sharing your gifts?

I feel very lucky to have people in my life who see my unique inner spark and support me one hundred percent. They love and understand my inner compass and always cheer me on. I encourage you to reach out to your network. Be brave, get some feedback on your One Thing, and get started. You might get the unwavering support and valuable insight you've always needed.

They might even ask you what your second or third thing was, and it can spark amazing insightful conversation. Please note, *getting feedback is not asking for permission*. You don't need permission from anyone else to go after your dream. The feedback is meant to be a tool for you to gain insight on your strengths and anchor your belief that you can get there.

Having several trusted companions along the way who believe in your vision is so valuable. I want you to feel as excited and empowered as possible as you continue through the exercises in this book.

You're doing great. Keep it up!

It's Time to Take Action Let's Get to Work!

The future belongs to those who believe
in the beauty of their dreams.

—ELEANOR ROOSEVELT

I n this second portion of the book, you explored the significance of beginning the pursuit of your goals and dreams before your children leave the nest. By recognizing the value of early preparation, this lays the foundation for a fun and fulfilling Empty Nest life. It's advantageous for so many reasons to embark on this journey now while your kids are still in high school instead of waiting until they are gone.

Starting to work on your Empty Nest dreams is a rare and golden opportunity. The years leading up to Empty Nesting provide a window of time to explore personal aspirations, make gradual adjustments, and cultivate new habits that align with your ideal future. Embracing this opportunity maximizes the potential for a smooth and purposeful transition.

I know several Empty Nesters who are struggling that simply didn't understand or prepare for how the transition would affect them. They didn't want to face the fact that their children were someday going to leave, so they procrastinated thinking about their Empty Nest future and developed Empty Nest Syndrome. But don't worry—that path isn't for you. It is just the beginning of your second half. You've got this!

Cultivating a distinct identity apart from your children does not mean you love them any less. Quite literally the opposite. By loving and nurturing your own needs alongside being a mother, you model positive behavior for your adult children. Take small steps and make incremental changes now to create a sense of progress, motivation, and excitement toward starting your One Thing. This early momentum will become a driving force to propel you toward a more rewarding life as an Empty Nester.

Whether you have predominantly worked in the home or balanced caregiving with a career, women often find it challenging to invest time in themselves. However, by embracing the future as a gift, you can carve out precious time to pour into your passions. Consider what you have put on hold and the dreams

> *By loving and nurturing your own needs alongside being a mother, you model positive behavior for your adult children.*

that you have yet to realize. Now is your moment to feel inspired and empowered to take action.

What do you think is possible for your next chapter? What small steps can you begin to take now to prepare yourself? How can you begin to make space to invest in you? Whether you have long desired to nurture your talent to paint, write, teach, start a business, or double down on your career, this is your time. It is just the beginning of the second half.

Many women, having spent the first half of their lives raising children, are hitting their professional stride later in life. According to *USA Today*, women-owned businesses have grown to nearly 13 million and account for 44 percent of all businesses. The average age of female founders is 45 and on the rise. And the retirement age of women has been steadily increasing, growing from 56 to 62 in just one year. Whatever your passion, it is not too late. This is going to be an incredible season for you!

My good friend, Cynthia Bentzen-Mercer, author of *Now, Near, Next*, encourages women to "start working on their futures today."[48] She works with her clients to build clarity around their core values and unique sense of purpose. With that as a foundation, Bentzen-Mercer suggests identifying one's natural talents, the "thoughts, feelings, and behaviors that are spontaneous, result in excellence, and bring intrinsic satisfaction."[49] What is your One Thing that fills your cup, you do better than most, and comes naturally to you?

Bentzen-Mercer's evidence-based methodology for defining and moving toward what's next is based on a two-thirds, one-third equation, which aligns beautifully to preparing for an Empty Nest.[50] She suggests spending two-thirds of the time leading up to your *next* making slow and steady progress, taking steps at a pace that fits within your current demands. This could be researching an area of interest, listening to podcasts, taking a class, updating your résumé, etc. The goal is to create forward momentum, even if you are only investing in yourself seven minutes a day.

In the final third of your timeline to your *next*, for example, when your last child approaches their senior year, it is time to accelerate. Bentzen-Mercer suggests the time leading up to executing your *next* requires increased focus and investment of time. This is a perfect opportunity to begin modeling resiliency, self-actualization, and independence to your youngest, who too will begin their own exploration in the near future.

Remember, one is better than zero. Progress is better than perfection. Consistency is key. By working on your One Thing, it will give you something to nurture and develop as your house grows emptier. This sets a positive example for your children, creating a legacy of self-love and fulfillment for them to model in their own lives.

You've engaged in self-reflection and identified something you currently love and want to do. Next, you will craft a game plan for how you will achieve that. When you actively begin working toward the dreams you are passionate about, you will experience increased happiness, fulfillment, and a greater sense of purpose—perfect emotions to be feeling as you get closer to your Empty Nest years. These positive emotions will carry over into your future, creating a more joyful and satisfying experience for everyone. Your Empty Nest can be one of the most fun and rewarding chapters in your life if you prepare for it. I promise.

Engaging in self-reflection is critical before you can start to define what your future will look like. It helps you identify where you are today, how far you have come, and what you want next. Remember, you are the author of your own story. It can look any way you want. I want you to design your next best chapter so you are extremely excited to get out of bed every day and work on your One Thing. I don't want this to be another thing you thought about doing and didn't. Working on your One Thing is going to positively impact your future in a multitude of ways. Let's get to the third part of the book and step into your future.

Chapter 14 Reflection Exercise

For the last exercise of section 2, take a few minutes to reread your answers from chapters 8 through 13. Having this insight and perspective fresh in your mind will help you easily absorb and apply the framework taught in the upcoming final chapters.

As you move toward a future filled with new opportunities, take a moment to be PRESENT:

 Picture your blank canvas symbolizing your new phase of life.

 Rediscover your FLOW state moments.

 Exchange each perceived limitation with a creative solution, and FLIP it.

 Support yourself as you would a best friend.

 Empower your future self by taking action now.

 Nurture your One Thing, and visualize life once you've accomplished it.

 Treat yourself with grace as your emotions ebb and flow.

Section 3 is all about taking action and creating a future for yourself, not tethered to the past, but aligned with a new destiny.

Let's get crystal clear on how you want your life to look in the near future and make a plan to get there. Make a personal commitment to see this next section through to the end. You'll be so glad you did.

I'm excited for you and I can't wait to witness your transformation.

SECTION III

Future

CHAPTER 15

Your Game Plan for Success
Action Is the Greatest Teacher

Making a plan for your dreams is the compass
that guides you towards their realization.

—TONY ROBBINS

I n section 1, you took a long look back at your incredible journey as a mother, acknowledged all the magical mini moments you've created for your family, and gained precious feedback from your children. In section 2, you reconnected to your current dreams and desires, learned the valuable lesson of letting go of limiting thoughts and beliefs, and cleared the canvas to make room for your soul whispers. I hope by now you've proven to yourself that your passions are indeed worthy and worth achieving.

Looking back at the significant moments you've had as a mother elevated the way you view possibilities for yourself in the future. Plus, getting positive feedback from your children filled with memories they love about you helped raise your vibration and self-awareness. It literally changed your brain chemistry!

Focusing on all the good in your life from an empowered perspective also allowed you to identify a few things that needed adjusting in your life without harsh self-judgment or criticism. It is easier to fix what's necessary and move forward in a more empowered way when you're feeling better about yourself.

Your passions are indeed worth achieving.

You assessed where you are in the present moment, and you picked your One Thing that will have a big impact on your future. You also determined if you are listening to your inner critic more than your inner compass, and you quieted that noise down with support from a friend. So many good things! You are now ready to create your next best chapter from a position of clarity, courage, and confidence.

Recognizing the substantial amount of love, energy, and time you invested during the prime years of raising your children is crucial. *You've been a mother for a really long time and should be proud of what you have done for your family.* However, as they start venturing out on their own, you will find you have more time for you and a newfound reservoir of untapped potential. This portion of the book aims to guide, inspire, and help you develop your own incredible, well-thought-out game plan for your Empty Nest years. Beginning to work on it now, before your children leave the nest, will infuse a new sense of purpose into your life, and help channel some of that love and energy back into you.

In this transformative chapter, you will apply the insight and knowledge you've gained and take action toward fulfilling your dreams by following a framework for creating an effective game plan. A map to the future you.

Your abundant, fulfilling life is waiting, and you never know where it might lead you. Let's get you started.

ESTABLISH YOUR GAME PLAN

At this point, creating a game plan that outlines the individual components and steps to achieve your One Thing is essential. A game plan is a visual guide to get you from where you are to where you want to be. It's a clear overview of what needs to be done, how it will be accomplished, what specific actions need to be taken, and what your desired result looks like. The process of creating this involves shifting from merely *thinking about* your desired outcome to defining what needs to be done and *taking action*. Yes, this will take work, but it's the fun kind of work.

Take a minute to get clear on your goals and define what a successful outcome looks like for you. When I was in my twenties, for example, a successful singing career might have looked like being the next Whitney Houston. *Lol.*

Now that I'm older and can define what success means to me, I would be happy singing a few of my songs for our family around a campfire at our cabin and just having fun. Success for me means having the courage to take a leap of faith and sing for my family despite the fear I may feel inside.

As we age, the definition of success shifts and is based more on our terms of what truly fills us up. Ask yourself, "What fulfills me on a soul level? And why do I want to achieve this One Thing?" Knowing *why* will help you stay the course, even on the days when you don't want to do the work.

Take time to reflect on your deepest desires, identify what truly brings you joy, and envision the life you want to lead when your children aren't around every day. And remember, starting with your One Thing is a good idea. I'm sure you have a lot of things you want to do in your Empty Nest, but let's start with one, cultivate that, and see where it naturally leads you. I promise, whatever your One Thing is, it has many components to it and will keep you very busy.

For example, if you want to write a book like I did, you will have to write an outline, research the market, decide whether to self-publish or find a publisher, get a book cover designer, edit, promote and sell it, etc. Writing a book actually made me learn so many new skills. It is such a multifaceted endeavor. It was a great place for me to start, and whatever you pick will be a great starting point for you, too.

In author Anthony Damaschino's book, *The Empty Nest Blueprint,* he discusses how a solid game plan begins with having a clear end goal in sight from the moment you start.[51] He emphasizes the empowering process of visualizing and mentally rehearsing your desired future when designing your detailed game plan. Much like an athlete before a big game or a speaker about to go on stage, visualizing what you want for your future makes it seem more achievable and gives you a sense of control.

Through a series of exercises, Damaschino directs his readers to document the future they want to create and has them visualize themselves living it. Not only does he have them visualize their future, but he then has them tie a strong emotion to it. They feel like they have already achieved their goals, and their emotions become elevated. This higher state of emotion is what anchors the subconscious to the belief that their vision is truly possible.

By feeling that you are already living your future, your brain will go into action to start attracting more of what you are envisioning for your life. So smart. Once you visualize your future and really "feel" the emotions attached to it, this significantly enhances your chances for achieving your goal. Damaschino emphasizes that many of his clients have repeatedly achieved their Empty Nest goals by applying this one technique. He is a great example of someone living their best Empty Nest life, and teaching others to do the same.

CULTIVATING A NEW CHAPTER

There are so many incredible stories about Empty Nesters cultivating a new passion project in their forties, fifties, and beyond. When they get clear on what they want in their lives and take the time to define that, magic starts to happen. And it will for you too!

Vera Wang is a great example of someone who defined a new vision for herself in midlife. After her children left home, she found herself at a crossroads and decided to continue her passion for fashion by jumping into something completely unknown and brand-new: bridal wear. With a relentless commitment to her craft and belief in her vision, Vera Wang revolutionized the wedding industry with unique designs, modern elegance, innovative silhouettes, and luxurious fabrics, attracting brides from all over the world.

She also offered brides the opportunity to personalize their wedding gowns, allowing them to customize details such as the neckline, sleeve style, and embellishments to create a one-of-a-kind dress. She had so many celebrity endorsements that her designs came into the spotlight and cemented her reputation as a leading bridal designer. She started with bridal wear, became a household name, and then expanded into many other specialties, including ready-to-wear collections, accessories, fragrances, and home goods.[52]

Becoming the next Vera Wang doesn't have to be the goal, obviously, but it's an incredible example of someone who in midlife clearly defined what they wanted, had a singular focus, pursued it relentlessly, and achieved something beyond their wildest dreams! When she started in bridal fashion, she had no idea that she was also going to have a crystal and china collection, jewelry, handbags, and a signature fragrance as part of her offerings. She ping-ponged her way to a greater outcome than she initially envisioned. How cool is that?

GAME PLAN FOR SUCCESS

Defining your primary objective (your One Thing), outlining the necessary steps to get there, and establishing a timeline for execution is important to do before you begin.

Here's a real-life example of a friend of mine who created a detailed plan of what she wanted and is now crushing it in her Empty Nesting years.

Step One: Your One Thing

Let's say your One Thing is to start your own business. I will use Sweet Pea Ink Creative as an example. When Cristina knew she wanted to start her creative brand and web design business, she outlined and then followed these steps to success:

 Brand Identity
   o   *Branding colors, font, logo design, personal website, etc.*

Product/Service Development
- o *Define products and services, and establish pricing based on market research.*

Marketing and Sales
- o *Develop a marketing plan to reach her target audience through various channels.*
- o *Create sales strategies to acquire customers and generate revenue.*

Financial Planning
- o *Prepare a budget detailing her start-up costs, ongoing expenses, and revenue projections.*

Client acquisition and management
- o *Develop a system for onboarding clients, and meet mutually agreed-upon deliverables.*
- o *Provide excellent customer service to retain clients and generate referrals.*

Personal work-life balance
- o *Prioritize self-care, and establish boundaries to maintain a healthy work-life balance.*
- o *Proactively plan for growth and scaling, and consider hiring a small team at the right time.*

But more importantly, I believe she is successful and sought after because before she designed the fundamentals of her business, she took time to precisely define who her ideal clients were and how she could best serve them. She got very specific about what her uniqueness was, what she could offer clients, what her clients needed (even if they didn't know it), and how she could best bring their brand to life. With this mindset, the rest of the business plan unfolded easily. She launched her business and instantly had full-time clients partner with her at the highest level. This is a great example of how someone launched an incredibly successful business in a short amount of time by following our Ten Cs game plan for success method. By defining all aspects of her game plan and working through each required component, she ended up with a beautiful, well-thought-out, thriving business. But how did she do that? She spent a lot of time working on the most important component of her game plan: her SMART goals. Let's discuss this more.

In their 1981 article, George Doran, Arthur Miller, and James Cunningham introduced the simple yet brilliant concept of SMART goals, aiming to help individuals set clear objectives they are more likely to achieve. SMART goals enhance focus, increase motivation, track progress, and help the individual stay motivated—all of which increase the likelihood of successful goal attainment. SMART goals empower individuals to stay consistent and make tangible progress toward their aspirations and dreams. Let's delve into what each letter in SMART signifies.

Specific. Goals should be clear and specific, avoiding ambiguity. They should answer the questions of who, what, where, when, and why.

Measurable. Goals should be quantifiable and measurable so that progress and milestones can be tracked.

Achievable. Goals should be realistic and attainable, considering the resources and constraints at hand.

Relevant. Goals should be relevant and align with the overall objective of the individual.

Time-bound. Goals should have a defined timeline or deadline for completion, providing a sense of urgency and motivation to work toward achieving them within a specified time frame.[53]

Using SMART goals when starting a new project allows you to take intentional action, track your progress, and celebrate milestones along the way. Using SMART goals while you start your new project, whatever it might be, greatly increases your chances for success and provides you with a map back to the road if you deviate from the path. Your game plan can act as a well-designed signal to your future self that you're on your way!

Remember to assess the resources you have available to you, such as financial, educational, or social support, and identify any gaps that need to be addressed. Building a network of individuals who can provide guidance, encouragement, and accountability can significantly enhance your journey toward personal fulfillment. And who knows, you might just meet someone that needs a little love and support from you, too.

An effective game plan serves as a road map to guide you toward the dream you have created for your future—providing clarity, direction, and motivation to create your best future one step at a time. It clears a path to get started by providing structure and guidance as you navigate this powerful transformation. You will have a map with the individual steps required to make your dream a reality. Don't let this part be overwhelming. It should be simple and effective, not overly detailed and complicated. Let's dive in.

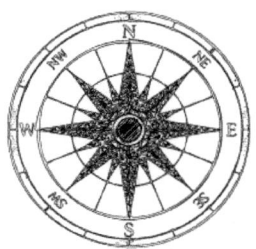

Chapter 15 Reflection Exercise

The time is here! You are going to design an actionable game plan for achieving your One Thing. You will define the essential components, actionable steps, and SMART goals for your Empty Nest game plan. It will serve as a guiding document for you that provides clarity, direction, and structure. Additionally, it's important to also get really clear on what a successful outcome means to you. Don't look outside yourself for this. Close your eyes and visualize what your personal success outcome looks and feels like to you. It feels good, doesn't it?

Take Anthony's advice. Attach a powerful positive emotion to your visualized outcome so you can really see it, feel it, and believe it! This is going to take some time, so please don't feel rushed. Work at a pace that is comfortable for you.

To get started, let's define your "game plan for success" and apply some SMART goals to your plan.

1. Specific:

What exactly are you trying to accomplish? What is your One Thing you are working on? What is your desired outcome? Do you want to:

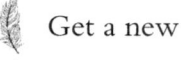 Get a new job?

Start a business?

Move to a new house or city?

Travel the world?

Learn a new skill or hobby?

Expand your friend group to include people that share your new interests?

Get your finances under control?

These are all examples of noteworthy goals. I can't wait to hear about what *you* picked personally! I'm so excited for you. Please share in our community on all things social @ TheEmptyNesterClub if you feel comfortable, and use the hashtag #OneThing or #GamePlan.

When your goals are specific, you can then take focused intentional action. You are more likely to achieve the desired outcome when you get detailed with your goals.

2. Measurable:

How will you measure what you are doing? How will you assess your achievements? Here are a few examples of my measurable goals I created when I started writing my book:

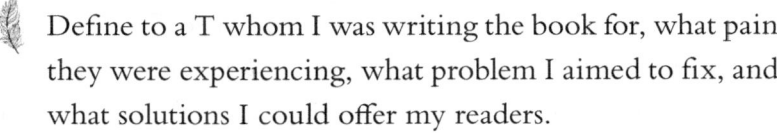 Define to a T whom I was writing the book for, what pain they were experiencing, what problem I aimed to fix, and what solutions I could offer my readers.

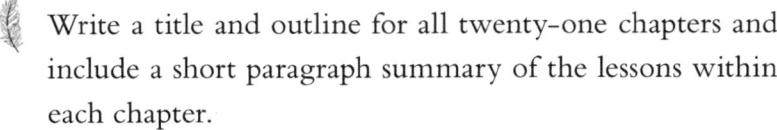 Write a title and outline for all twenty-one chapters and include a short paragraph summary of the lessons within each chapter.

Decide how each chapter would flow. What repeatable components does each chapter have? For example, in my current book, each chapter follows this general outline: I have a title, a quote, a lesson I teach through either a personal story or someone else's story, research statistics, and then insightful ideas on how the reader can incorporate what they just learned. I follow this method within every chapter for consistency and clarity.

Timeblock my schedule to include two to three hours per day for writing, editing, and working on all things branding.

Stay balanced and healthy. Currently, my personal care is extra important to me, so I have that time blocked into my schedule in the morning. Taking care of myself first makes me a more creative writer, keeps me on task, and better equips me to serve my audience.

Whatever your goal is, making it measurable will allow you to track your progress, make adjustments if necessary, and keep you motivated.

3. Attainable:

With the tools that you have, can you reach your goal? Is it doable? If not, what do you need to do in order to make it attainable? For example, if you are trying to get more involved in fundraising during your Empty Nesting years, how do you start?

Let's say you want to raise funds to purchase winter coats for children in need.

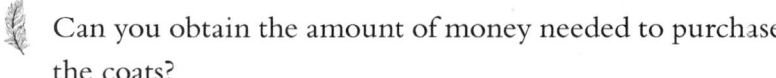 Can you obtain the amount of money needed to purchase the coats?

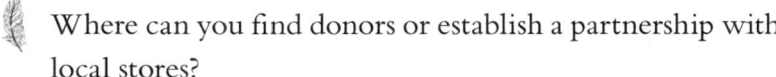 Where can you find donors or establish a partnership with local stores?

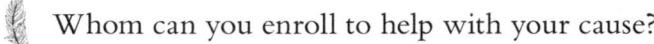 Whom can you enroll to help with your cause?

How can you find engaged sponsors to support you, and what can you do for them in return?

Achieving smaller goals will boost your confidence and belief in your ability to accomplish larger goals in the future. This positive reinforcement is important for long-term success, so make sure your first goal is attainable.

4. Realistic:

What do you want to achieve by working on this One Thing, and are your expectations realistic? Can you meet the goals you defined for yourself based on your current level of knowledge, time available, and daily circumstances? Knowing *why* you want to achieve your goals will also help you get more clear on the *how*. Let's use the example of getting your finances under control.

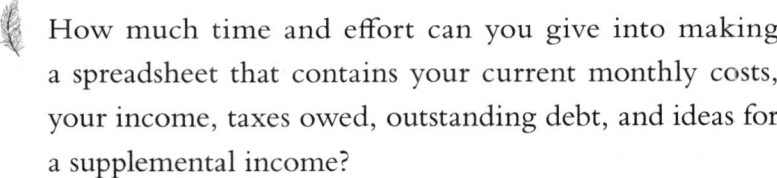 How much time and effort can you give into making a spreadsheet that contains your current monthly costs, your income, taxes owed, outstanding debt, and ideas for a supplemental income?

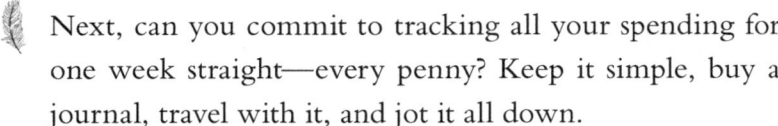 Next, can you commit to tracking all your spending for one week straight—every penny? Keep it simple, buy a journal, travel with it, and jot it all down.

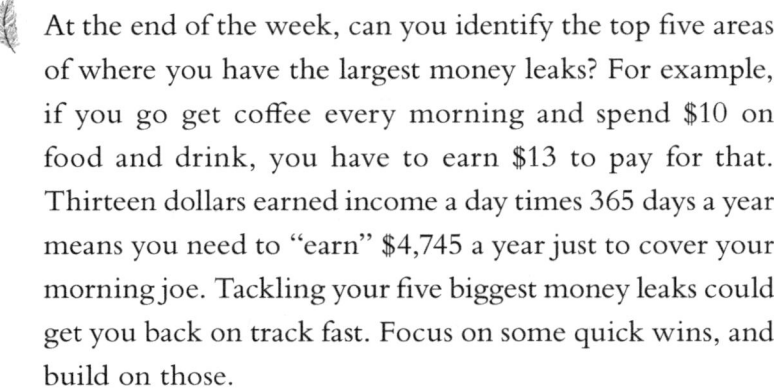 At the end of the week, can you identify the top five areas of where you have the largest money leaks? For example, if you go get coffee every morning and spend $10 on food and drink, you have to earn $13 to pay for that. Thirteen dollars earned income a day times 365 days a year means you need to "earn" $4,745 a year just to cover your morning joe. Tackling your five biggest money leaks could get you back on track fast. Focus on some quick wins, and build on those.

If the objective is not realistic, what do you need to do to make it so, or do you need to adjust the goal completely? Could you enlist the help of an expert to gain clarity?

I love it when people dream big, but to achieve big dreams, you have to start small. Success is in the details. Big goals are realized when broken down into bite-sized baby steps taken consistently over time. Make sure your goals are realistic, and build from there.

5. Timely:

What is the timeline to meet your goals? Work backward. Start with what date you want to achieve your goal by and back into that date with your detailed plan. Create an outline for the milestones that need to be reached, and give them a date. This is one of the most important components to goal setting.

An example of this could be preparing for a race:

In twelve months, I will run my first half-marathon.

 I will study how to train for this and break down the steps required working backward from the race date.

 I will build in proper nutrition and sleep, follow a weekly running schedule, and find an accountability partner.

 My goal is to complete the marathon in under five hours. To do this, I will schedule measurable milestones to hit, review my progress every week, and adjust my goal accordingly.

Backward planning helps you identify when each milestone needs to get done. When you attach a timeline to a goal, that will keep you on track and create a sense of urgency to achieve what you desire. You should be proud that you are going to take action on a dream you've had for a long time. Remember, start small so you can stack up some early successes. If you do that, you will be more consistent with your actions. I'm so excited to see what you create for yourself. You deserve it! Next, let's discuss how to get started in the right way so you never want to quit ever again.

CHAPTER 16

Baby Steps
Consistency over Time is Powerful

Consistency is the mother of mastery.

—ROBIN SHARMA

Making a plan is one thing, but actually doing the work consistently is an entirely different ball game. We've all started something only to quit shortly after. It makes us feel bad about ourselves, and oftentimes we end up abandoning our plan completely. But if we truly understood the power of small, consistent effort over time, and based success on that, it would be quite a different story. By starting small, we lay the foundation for significant payoffs in the long run. Each tiny step forward brings us closer to the rewards that await us on the path to fulfilling our deepest desires. It's the accumulation of seemingly insignificant moments that weave the grand tapestry of our success.

Now that you have a game plan created for what to do and how to do it, the next step is to talk about your new routines and habits that develop as you make progress toward your goal. Success is not about perfection. It never has been. We all miss the mark sometimes, and that's okay. You don't need to follow your plan 100 percent of the time to be successful. You just need to stay on track, be consistent, measure your progress, and make adjustments along the way. Let's review what a successful routine could look like for you.

Growordie on TikTok talks about how he changed his entire life by implementing four daily routines: early mornings, mornings, afternoons, and evenings, with each consisting of five attainable goals. He wrote down everything he did and didn't do for months with *zero* judgment. In his first month, he discovered he was only completing his evening routine about 50 percent of the time. On a grading scale, we all know that's an F! Instead of defining it as a failure, he acknowledged where he was at and didn't give up.

Success is not about perfection. It never has been.

He made a simple adjustment to his attitude and expectations and chose to think more positively. He reminded himself, "These are just new skills I'm not good at yet. It's fine. No big deal."[54] Because he embodied this new mindset, stuck with it, and applied this practice over time, he's now consistently in the 80 percentile range for each routine every month. He's following the Pareto principle, better known as the 80/20 rule. But here's what's so smart about his unique approach. He never shoots for 100 percent. Ever. He knows he's going to fall short if that's the goal, and that's not what he's growing toward.

What is he doing differently? His new 100 percent is now 80 percent. Brilliant. When you look at it this way, it's fascinating what we could accomplish in a short period of time if we stop beating ourselves up and instead choose to show up consistently. That's real success. The goal is to always be consistent, not perfect. Doing something 80 percent of the time over one year, he will have completed all four of these routines 292 times out of 365 days. Multiply that by 4, and his daily habits have been performed over 1,168 times in one year! If he had quit, it would be 0. Compound that over several years, and you can master anything.

Setbacks are going to happen, but how you bounce back from them is what matters. It is okay and normal to have breakdowns on the way to your breakthrough. You should expect them. Activating new parts of yourself will take some time to master, but it's good for your personal growth.

Here's why his method works. In his process, there are two keys to long-term success that you can apply to your current goals; setting proper expectations (shooting for 80 percent) and consistently showing up imperfectly (even

> *It is okay to have breakdowns on the way to your breakthrough.*

when he's not perfect; he keeps going). He's mastered the art of the compound effect, one of my favorite concepts in the world. Let's talk a bit more about this.

CHOOSE CONSISTENCY OVER PERFECTION

In his *NYT* best-selling book *The Compound Effect,* author Darren Hardy talks about the power of small, consistent actions compounding over time to transform ordinary efforts into extraordinary results. He says, "You will never change your life until you change something you do daily."[55] That's powerful. Can't argue with that.

We all can make changes to things we do, but can we commit to doing it daily, even if it's not our very best? Showing up daily has a cumulative effect on your goals. It's *time* that polishes the coal into a diamond, not extra effort. Showing up consistently can take some getting used to if your past pattern has been starting, stopping, and starting over and over again. There's so much freedom when you jump off that merry-go-round.

Make consistent, compounded effort toward your goal, and it will work for you. Every time.

Now that you have a plan and your baby steps are manageable, keep moving forward and don't stop. If you mess up, just think of it like you took a wrong exit off of the freeway. No shame clouds! Turn right back around, get back on the freeway, and keep moving forward. Make consistent, compounded effort toward your goal, and it will work for you. Every time.

Understanding why we make the choices we do and what our current daily habits look like are crucial for this next step. It will keep you consistent with your plan and help you achieve your ultimate goal. Let's dissect this.

In his *NYT* best-selling book *Atomic Habits*, author James Clear explains the concept of habit formation and provides practical strategies for creating positive change in your life.[56] He deconstructs the concept of the habit loop I referenced earlier, which consists of:

 **Cue**

Craving

Response

Reward

By understanding this loop, you can manipulate it to your advantage and improve any habit you want. Clear suggests that you can trick your brain by making the cues for positive habits simpler and more obvious, and the cues for negative habits more difficult and less visible.[57]

This was fascinating to me, so I applied his habit loop concept to help me start running again. I love to run, but during the pandemic, I stopped. I didn't know why I stopped until I understood the *craving* within my habit loop had changed. By implementing his techniques, I started running again in a fairly short period of time. I had to learn the cue for my behavior, the craving behind it, the response I had to the craving, and the reward I was seeking.

Here is an example of my pre-pandemic running habit loop:

I would see my workout shoes (cue). It made me remember the thrill I got from running (crave). I would put on my workout shoes and go for a run (response). I felt great after completing my run (reward).

However, during the pandemic, something had changed in my habit loop. My usual reward of feeling fit and getting stronger wasn't enough to make me take action. There are clues in your habit loops. If you're not doing something you want to do, find out where your habit loop is disrupted. For me, during the pandemic, my *craving* had changed, so the typical reward I got from running no longer matched my new craving. Safety and comfort was what I was craving, not the exhilaration and excitement a long run used to give me.

Once I figured out where my habit loop had changed, it was easy to fix. I stopped saying, "I need to start running three miles every day," which would trigger my brain to go on high alert because it was too big of a challenge at the time. When I figured out I was craving comfort, I started with a small, baby step–sized goal that wouldn't make my brain too uncomfortable. I really wanted to start running again, but the old way I went about it wasn't going to work.

In order to change my habit loop, I did exactly what his book suggests. He calls it the two-minute rule. The idea is to make your habits so easy to start that you can't say no to them. By starting with a very small action that takes less than two minutes, your brain won't freak out and will accept the slight change. It seemed silly to me at first, but I followed this to a T. On the first night, I simply placed my shoes and workout clothes by my bed and put them on first thing in the morning. That's it. I did not go for a walk or a run that day. My brain could handle putting on my shoes and clothes. Minimal threat.

Cue—my shoes and clothes

Craving—to feel safe

Response—I got dressed in my workout clothes and shoes

Reward—I felt comfortable

The next day, I built from there. My goal was to walk outside for two minutes. Okay. My brain was comfortable with that. Baby steps. On the third day, I ran for one minute and ended up walking for another twenty-nine! This was a great start. One I could build on. On the fourth day, I ran for two minutes, and so on. By starting with an easy goal and growing from there, I didn't set alarms off in my brain about running three miles, which felt impossible at the time because I had taken so much time off from running. These baby steps were easy and comfortable, and they made me want to progress a little more every day. I looked forward to achieving these mini wins, and pretty soon, I reached my goal of running three miles three times a week.

It was fascinating to witness this process at work, because it seemed so simple. Reverse engineer the way you approach your habits. Smart. Once I did this consistently for a few weeks, my craving for the exhilaration and excitement of running returned too! I was so happy I didn't have to force it. It happened naturally. I had rewired my habit loop, and I couldn't wait to apply this to so many other areas of my life. I'm grateful I now understand the two-minute rule principle and how to start anything new without sabotaging my results like I used to in the past. Thank you, Mr. James Clear. You're a genius.

By tricking your brain, breaking down new goals into the smallest denominator possible, and building from there, you are more likely to show up every day with less effort and resistance. Start small and build on that bit by bit with daily, bite-sized goals, and see where you are in a month. This method can work in any area of your life where you want to create lasting change. The two-minute rule is the perfect principle to ensure you will take consistent action on your One Thing. No more starting and stopping things and breaking promises to yourself, okay? Over time that can really affect your self-esteem, and that's no fun.

Now that you understand why it's been so easy to quit in the past, don't beat yourself up. Learn from it. It wasn't you or your lack of willpower. Your brain just needs to start with smaller tasks, have some easy wins, and consistently build on those over time. And now that you know this, you can hack any habit loop. Easy peasy.

Can your current habits help you reach your goals? Or are they contributing to results you don't want? Good habits are essential to your success. Take a look at your habits, what you are attracting, and what results you are getting so you can assess if you are in a good position to maintain the new life you want to create. Staying consistent and working on your future with good habits in place is the best thing you can do to prepare for your Empty Nest. Believe that you can create whatever you want for your future. You got this.

Chapter 16 Reflection Exercise

For this next exercise, I invite you to adopt a mindset that will be beneficial for this growth period: a flexible mindset. This will allow you to adapt to change as new information comes at you, which fosters innovation and progress. On the other hand, a rigid mindset resists change and often leads to missed opportunities for learning and improvement. So make sure you're going into this next process with a flexible mindset, just like Growordie on TikTok does. Eighty percent is your new 100 percent, and adjustments are key for learning.

Grab your journal and make a list of the new, actionable "baby steps" you will to take toward your game plan and SMART goals. Make sure they are bite-sized so you can ensure you'll do them and build on your small wins. Remember, consistent effort over compounded time leads to success, not extra effort. Pick one actionable step you will take today toward one small, attainable goal. Apply the "putting on your running shoes" concept to the first step you need to take for your desired result. Make sure you are aware of what you are currently craving, because satisfying your current cravings will determine your success.

What's the one new goal or habit I will achieve today?

 What cue will I put into place to start this process?

- **Cue:** *This is the trigger that initiates the behavior. It is a signal that prompts your brain to start a particular habit.*

 What am I craving? Why did I pick this goal?

- **Craving:** *After the cue, there is a feeling of desire or craving for the reward associated with the habit. This craving is what motivates you to act. Sidenote—craving novelty, excitement, or peaceful rest are three very different things, so make sure you know what your current needs are. Once you know what you need and crave in this moment, you can turn that baby step into success. This will allow you to maintain your new rhythm in life with much less effort.*

 What response will I have, and what will I do when I see my cue?

- **Response:** *This is the actual behavior or action that you will take in response to the cue. Make sure this is realistic, doable, and won't trigger alarms in your brain that think you are making too big of a change. Keep it small and simple.*

 What reward will I feel once I finish my new goal or habit?

- **Reward:** *The reward is the outcome or benefit that you gain from performing the habit. It satisfies the craving and reinforces the habit loop.*

By understanding and manipulating the four elements of a habit loop—the cue, craving, response, and reward—you can consistently and effectively build new habits or break old ones. Doing new things will cause your daily rhythms to change, and that's good. Change can feel threatening at first, but if you lean into it, stick with it, and consistently show up, it will positively affect your life in so many areas. Build on your baby steps and celebrate your progress. It will help you maintain the new rhythm in life that you are creating for your best Empty Nest.

Maintaining Your New Rhythm
Lean into the Discomfort

Embrace the discomfort of a new rhythm, for within it lies
the potential for the most joyful transformation of your life.

—BRENÉ BROWN

E mbracing a new rhythm in your life can be exciting and uncomfortable at first, especially when you try new things and work hard to do them consistently. Not only are you adjusting to your ever-changing daily routines as your children start to leave the nest, but you are also acclimating to a new

You are growing forward and glowing up.

rhythm that arises when you pursue new goals. It's a double whammy, and it can take some getting used to. You are growing forward and glowing up. Good for you! Consistently taking baby steps forward is a great goal, and from doing this, a new daily rhythm will emerge for you that will organically align with your life.

You've taken courageous first steps to turn your goal into a reality. Now it's time to delve into the importance of maintaining this new rhythm and overcoming old behaviors and beliefs that might pop up. In this chapter, we will explore strategies to confront self-sabotage, embrace discomfort, streamline your new schedule, and keep the momentum going.

Change often brings discomfort and takes you out of your comfort zone. However, it's important to recognize that discomfort is a natural part of change. Embrace it as a sign that you are stretching yourself and stepping into new territory. It's a sign that you are learning and growing. Feeling uncomfortable doesn't mean you are doing something wrong. It's a good thing.

Even after crafting a game plan for your future and working on new goals, that inner critic may rear its ugly head once again, tempting you to halt your progress and go back to your old ways of thinking and being. Recognize that this inner voice, as we previously discussed, is just your brain expressing fear of change and internal self-doubt. So don't listen to what it's saying. Challenge it by acknowledging your new way of thinking, remind yourself of the reasons why you got started, and just keep showing up to do the work. Replacing self-sabotaging thoughts with positive affirmations reinforces your commitment to personal growth. And your understanding of your current habit loops is very important during this process. Embrace the challenge, and trust in your ability to adapt and thrive in your new rhythm of life.

In the book *The Big Leap* by Gay Hendricks, she talks about staying in your zone of excellence versus moving into your zone of genius, which we discussed briefly in chapter 9.[58] Temptation can be strong to remain in your zone of excellence, probably where you've been living much of your life up to today. It's also where family, friends, and organizations want you to stay. You're predictable there, reliable, and provide them a steady supply of everything they thrive on. But remember, this is the time for you to focus on your dreams, because that reward is going to feel so good. That deep, sacred part of your soul doesn't want to stay in the zone of excellence anymore. It wants to leap into your zone of genius and express your gifts to the fullest.

> *Your Zone of Genius is where you feel most aligned with your true self and calling. It's where the magic starts to happen.*

Your zone of genius is where you feel most aligned with your true self and calling. It's where the magic starts to happen. You are moving into your zone of genius, so it's important to keep growing and maintaining your new rhythm. Don't shy away from it. Your new rhythm will start to feel comfortable as you consistently show up day after day. These changes might feel uncomfortable for your family, friends, and the organizations you impact. But trust me. If you lean into it and trust it, you will have a greater outcome than you could have ever imagined. Your zone of genius is calling you. It always has been.

This might be a good time for you to revisit the Clear the Canvas chapter and reassess each one of your puzzle piece priorities. Now that you have begun to work on your One Thing and are visibly changing to your outside world, take inventory of your priorities. Have some become more important, less important, or completely fallen off the list? Make sure your priorities are in order and you are spending a good amount of time doing things you love to do. It is important for this next chapter of your life.

Let's take a deeper dive into where all of your time is going and what you can do about it so you can intentionally maximize and maintain your new rhythm in life. This is great preparation work for your Empty Nest.

APPLY THE SOS MODEL

I recently completed Cherylanne Skolnicki's incredible "Brilliant Balance Revive" course.[59] I highly recommend it for anyone wanting to refresh their habits, release expectations, and redesign the rhythm of their week. This course helped me define my top priorities and maximize how I schedule my time. It completely changed my life. It's one of the best, most-well-thought-out courses I have taken.

One of my favorite lessons is in her fourth pillar (there are nine in total). She's coined a process called The SOS Model— Stop, Offload, and Simplify—which allows you to easily identify areas in your schedule that can be improved or removed completely. In this section of her program, you take an in-depth look at your life for seven straight days, logging what you spend your time doing every half hour, from 7:00 a.m. until 10:00 p.m. Then you have to color-code each bucket of time on your spreadsheet as either "simplify," "stop doing," "have to do," "need to offload," or "love to do." This was such an eye-opening exercise and so worth the effort because it allowed me to see where all of my time was going—good, bad, and opportunities for improvement. Netflix, anyone?

After your weekly log is complete, you then apply the SOS Model to your results. What do you need to Stop doing completely? What tasks can you Offload to someone else to handle? And what can you Simplify or batch together to use your time more efficiently? For example, I was shocked by how much time I was wasting going to the grocery store every single day, sometimes twice a day if I forgot something. I now create a detailed shopping list for my week and batch-shop on Mondays, and it's given me back four to five hours of time in my week! That one change provided me with much-needed extra time to write. I now have a streamlined approach for creating my weekly schedule, and I love it. I took back control, and the payoffs have been huge.

When you think about the rhythm of your week in this phase of life, can you see how applying the SOS Model to your schedule could help you achieve your goals more quickly? What tasks can you offload to someone else to handle so you can get more time back in your week? Are there any tasks you can completely stop doing and replace with something else?

This was such a powerful exercise for me because I thought I was managing my Almost Empty Nest time pretty well, and surprise! I discovered I was not. After I applied the SOS Model to my week, got rid of the activities that were draining me and had no value, and replaced them with things that brought me joy, I felt like I was on top of the world (and my schedule). I highly encourage you to check out her courses. They truly are *brilliant*.

Transitioning to an Empty Nest means a significant shift in your daily routines, but with a little intentionality, you can master this change and easily maintain your new rhythm. When your kids leave the nest, your daily life will change for sure, but it also frees up space for you to explore new interests, activities, and passions that bring you joy and fulfillment, and the courage to get rid of the ones that don't. When you do this, it opens up so much time for you to focus on things you love to do. Trust that your life is about to enter a new chapter, and that can be exciting. You are redesigning your future to your liking and sticking to a new plan that lights you up from within.

When you find new friends that align with what you are interested in, it's almost as if the magic doubles.

And what better way to stay on track than to find a community that shares your same interests? When you find new friends that align with what you are interested in, it's almost as if the magic doubles. You support and encourage each other naturally. It's such an amazing time in life to connect with new, like-minded people or old friends who are at the same stage that you are. Let's talk about how to do that.

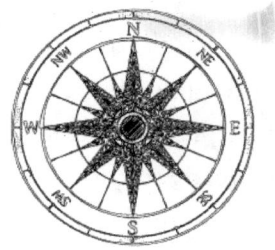

Chapter 17 Reflection Exercise

It's so important to embrace this new rhythm in your life, especially when you are trying new things before becoming an Empty Nester. You are working on new habits and goals, and that can feel unusual. But I promise that after a little bit of time, it will start to feel normal. Lean into the discomfort for now and keep going. One thing that I find helpful to do in case I feel myself slipping a bit is to interrupt the habit loop by adding one simple extra step: replacement.

 Cue

 Craving

 **Replacement**

 Response

 Reward

Having a craving but not responding to it means something is up. The chain is disrupted somewhere. Adding in a temporary replacement (a placeholder if you will) can help you unlock the freeze and take action. For example, if you see the cue for running, and your craving isn't strong enough to make you take action, maybe insert a temporary replacement such as listening to your favorite running playlist or doing a fifteen-minute yoga or stretch session to get ready to run. That little replacement just might be enough to get you going and move you into response mode: going for a run. Maybe you just needed a little push, and now you're ready to roll.

Here's how you do this:

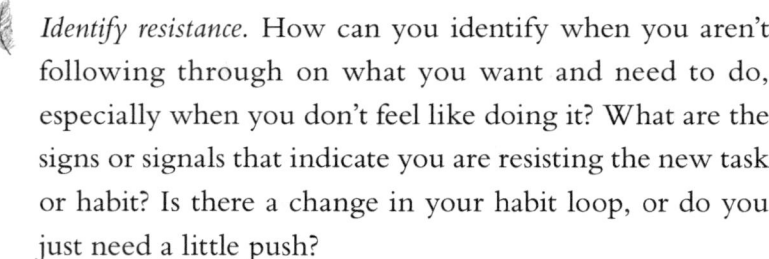

Identify resistance. How can you identify when you aren't following through on what you want and need to do, especially when you don't feel like doing it? What are the signs or signals that indicate you are resisting the new task or habit? Is there a change in your habit loop, or do you just need a little push?

Questioning your beliefs. When faced with resistance or lack of motivation, tune into your internal dialogue. What questions can you ask yourself to challenge your resistance and reaffirm your commitment before you get too far off track?

Interrupting your habit loop. How can you interrupt the habit loop between craving and response? Insert a *replacement* behavior before your desired response. Consider a specific strategy or technique that can help you hijack your habit loop in just the right area. What new action can you introduce to shift your mindset and behavior toward fulfilling your commitment, even when you don't feel like it?

SOS Model. What is something in your life that you can Stop, Offload, or Simplify that might help clear some things off your plate so you have a better chance of maintaining these new habits you have created? What do you no longer need to do so you can open up space for new goals and habits?

When you figure out how to lean into and maintain this new rhythm of life by hijacking your habits and applying the SOS Model, you will be so happy you did when you start to see your results. There are probably a lot of local communities you could tap into to keep your excitement and momentum going. It's great to go through this transformation with like-minded friends in your community. Let's talk about the importance of finding that.

CHAPTER 18

*Find Your Community
Your Tribe Is Calling*

*Find your tribe. Love them hard. Together, you can
create magic and manifest your shared vision.*

—MEL ROBBINS

W hen your children move out, social dynamics often
undergo significant changes. Days spent connecting
with other moms at practice, recitals, or end-of-year performances
are now few and far between. Maybe some of your friend groups
are starting to shift or move away. Or maybe you are beginning
to invest in new friendships. Connecting with new people who
share your vision for creating a fun and fulfilling Empty Nest
can be fun and refreshing. It's exciting to be around people who
share the same interests and hobbies that you do, and it's good
for your health as well.

Making connections with communities that share your same passions and goals is important for several reasons. According to the American Society of Training and Development, sharing a goal you have with someone can increase the chances of achieving it by up to 95 percent more than going at it alone.[60] Having a supportive community significantly increases your chances of success when embarking on new endeavors later in life. And research consistently shows the profound impact it can have on human well-being and personal fulfillment.

According to a study published in the *Journal of Experimental Social Psychology*, connecting with individuals who share our values, goals, and hobbies not only enhances our sense of belonging but also boosts our overall happiness and motivation.[61] The science of community highlights how these social connections can provide support, encouragement, and a sense of purpose, ultimately leading to improved mental health and a better quality of life.

The sense of belonging, encouragement, and resources that these communities provide can be invaluable as you pursue your passion project, start a small business, or master a new skill. These individuals have experienced or are currently going through similar transitions and challenges, making them uniquely positioned to provide you support and guidance. Sharing your stories and aspirations with your community creates a safe space where you can feel understood, validated, and encouraged. And your personal experiences will help them too.

I have recently begun to bond with a new group of Almost Empty Nesters and Empty Nesters online. We meet up once a month to discuss all things Empty Nesting. Even though I'm not quite an Empty Nester, it's been wonderful to hear about everyone's inspiring and amazing Empty Nest stories. They've given me so many ideas to add to my list of things to do. One of them was pickleball! Yes, I know. I'm late to the game, but they say it's a must. Recently, I reached out to this group to seek advice on how they made friends at this stage of life. They came back with some incredible ideas that I wanted to share with you. Here are some of their top suggestions:

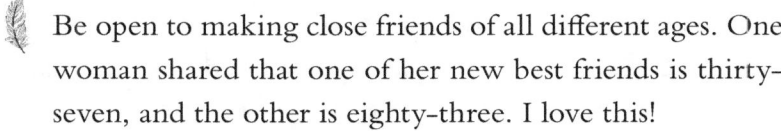

- Be open to making close friends of all different ages. One woman shared that one of her new best friends is thirty-seven, and the other is eighty-three. I love this!

- Reconnect with high school or college friends from the past. They're probably going through exactly what you are going through. It's so fun to laugh and reminisce about the good ol' times and support each other through this next chapter.

- Learn new group hobbies like pilates, pickleball, or yoga.

- Pick up an old hobby like golf, tennis, singing in a choir, or swimming. Masters Swimming groups are fun and have locations all over.

- Start a local Facebook group for moms of adult children. One Empty Nest mom has a group of 1,300 local members, and they have had forty meetup events. Such a great idea no matter where you live! Attend local events in your city, art museums, church, etc.

- Go to meetup.com, and check out some of the options there. They offer hiking groups, wine tasting, travel groups, etc.

THE BEAUTY OF A NEW TRIBE

Being part of a community that shares your values and Empty Nesting goals can be a powerful source of motivation. You will learn from their experiences, gain new perspectives, and be inspired by their achievements. And you'll probably be a great resource and source of inspiration for them too.

I have a friend who is sixty and has recently picked up her guitar again. She plays a few gigs around our music-lovin' mountain ski town. How cool is that! She's met so many new friends and is living out her Empty Nest dream. She finally inspired me to pick up a guitar after forty years of wanting to learn how to play. It's uncomfortable, but I'm going to stick with it in hopes of bringing one of the many songs I have written to life.

Another friend of mine, Sue Ball, was feeling lost and disconnected without the daily demands of parenting. She missed having a strong social circle and was looking for a way to connect with other Empty Nesters. She's always been drawn to the travel industry, so Sue and her husband started Sphera Travel. It's a collection of group travel offerings for Empty Nesters eager to explore new horizons. They help create unforgettable memories on amazing adventures with fellow Empty Nest explorers. Through their company, Sue and her husband have met hundreds of new couples and traveled all over the world together. Amazing.

In like-minded communities, you get to engage in mutually meaningful conversations and exchange incredible ideas about your shared passions. You can seek advice, share challenges, and even celebrate your victories together. These connections become a source of ongoing support, shared experiences, and can turn into lifelong friendships. I hope you branch out and find a group like this for yourself. It's nice to have something to look forward to that fills you up on a soul level.

Our existing friend groups can be a great source to draw from as well. Friendship pods that cross over with one another are so special. Within my hometown, I have a few core groups of friends, and it seems that within those friend groups, someone through someone knows everyone. It's amazing the possibility and power these friendship pods hold. I wish we all tapped into them more regularly.

> *It's nice to have something to look forward to that fills you up on a soul level.*

Last year, I wanted to get to know some of my friends' friends. I held a "Galentine" party at my house right after Valentine's day, and I asked each of my friends to invite one friend I didn't know. The evening was so fun, and I learned so much about people I had never met! What was great, though, is that I met a few authors that night and have stayed in touch with them. It's so nice to have local author friends I can go through this journey with. Ahhh, the blessing of the pods.

Chapter 18 Reflection Exercise

For this exercise, spend some time researching groups within your community that are doing what you want to do. Who else is on this journey with you, and how can you find them? If you can, hop online and see if there are any local meetup groups that share the same interests you have.

Additionally, call or email several friends, and let them know you are soon to be an Empty Nester and would love to connect with other people they know that share your interests, both new and old. Maybe you are ready to finally write a book and share your own story. See if one of your friends can introduce you to an author that would be willing to have coffee with you. The possibilities are endless.

Ask yourself these questions:

- What's one way I could get to know more people in my community who share my interests?

- Who might need to connect with me that I don't know yet? How can I put myself out there?

- Are any of these groups advertised in the local paper, library, or through a higher-ed school program?

- If there's not a group, can I start up my own?

And most importantly, how can I best serve this new community? "Life Gives to the Givers," as my good friend and author Joe Polish always says.

Make a list of a few ideas you have, and promise to take action on at least one or two. You will be so glad you did.

Future You

The Ripple Effect

Believe in the possibilities of creating an extraordinary future life for yourself, for it is within your power to make it a reality.

—ALBERT EINSTEIN

L et's pretend for a moment it's one year from now, and you have consistently worked on your game plan, Your One Thing, and achieved everything you set out to do. Think about all the ways your life has changed for the better. Do you feel more fulfilled? Content? Grateful? Excited?

When you think of your future self, are you filled with a sense of pride and accomplishment, not just for achieving your initial goal, but for the myriad of ways that lives have been elevated by the ripple effect of your actions? It could be that your book is now published, your guitar skills have improved, your new business is going well, or you have a lot of new friends. Life is good.

As your children begin to leave the nest, it's so important they continue to witness you pursuing your passions and chasing your dreams. Your friends and family will marvel at your transformation too, which could inspire them to start working on their own passion projects as well. When you intentionally create a new version of your life and start living from that energy, you will show up in ways that you haven't before, and it will have a major impact in every area of your life.

Take a look back at your top five soul whispers. Did taking action on your One Thing cause you to work on a few more things you love? Can you see how what began as a single choice has blossomed into a myriad of new experiences? The ripple effect of your actions has not only transformed your own life, but has touched the lives of those around you, creating a

There is so much joy in the journey.

web of inspiration and empowerment that extends far beyond what you could have ever imagined.

This journey is not just about reaching a destination but about embracing the transformative power of the process itself. Trust in the ripple effect of your actions. Have faith in the seeds you sow today and know that by working on your One Thing consistently, it will allow you to also work on a few others from your top five list. Action opens up a floodgate of possibilities and releases new creative energy within you. There is so much joy in the journey.

For example, when I chose to work on my book, I set aside learning guitar and writing songs. I focused solely on my One Thing. That worked for a while, but once my creativity was flowing again, I found it easier to pick up my guitar and write songs during my in-between moments because the resistance wasn't there anymore. I am now in the habit of tapping into my creativity on a regular basis and it feels amazing. Working on my One Thing caused such a beautiful domino effect in my life. I'm happy my husband and children got to witness these profound personal changes over the past two years, and I want the same for you.

Sometimes you just never know how big of a ripple effect you are going to make. A good friend of mine, Bill Decker, works with the incredible organization ShelterBox, and the ripple effect they have created is life-changing for many communities.

ShelterBox was founded to provide emergency shelter to people affected by disasters and humanitarian crises around the world.[62] What began as a small, simple project of the Rotary Club of Helston-Lizard in Cornwall, England grew to shelter more than 2 million people in more than 100 countries around the world to date. Little did those well-intentioned club members know that ShelterBox would become the largest Rotary Club project in the world, with affiliates in countries across the globe and the support of the Queen Consort of the United Kingdom as its royal patron.

That modest ripple that began in 2000 continues to impact communities at the very local level today. ShelterBox—having responded to the Philippines an average of two disasters per year over the last twenty years—approached local stakeholders in 2017 about building a local affiliate that would better empower the citizens of the Philippines to take charge of their own disaster preparedness and responses with the support of the global ShelterBox network and Rotary International. This effort acted as a regional and local force multiplier, activating a more broad volunteer and donor base within the communities themselves to efficiently and effectively respond to disasters. The model is under consideration for replication in several other frequently affected communities around the globe, with the intent of building resilience and improved capacity for managing disaster recoveries around the world. These are the ripples that can deliver profound change to vulnerable populations with multigenerational impact.[62] Incredible!

Embrace the butterfly effect in your life as you move through this process. Just like the flutter of a butterfly's wings can set off a chain reaction that leads to a hurricane on the other side of the world, the small steps you are taking today toward your dreams can create waves of change that ripple through your life in ways you never imagined. In the universe, every action, no matter how small, carries the potential to create a ripple effect that can possibly improve the entire world.

A simple but wonderful example of this is the Pay It Forward movement that started with a simple act of kindness and led to a chain reaction of generosity and goodwill. In 2014, a customer at a coffee shop in St. Petersburg, Florida started a Pay It Forward chain by paying for the coffee of the person in line behind them.[63] This small act of kindness sparked a chain reaction that lasted for over eleven hours, with 378 customers participating and paying for the orders of strangers behind them. When people observe others engaging in altruistic behavior, they are more likely to pay it forward and act generously toward others too. The Pay It Forward movement has gained momentum in recent years, with various initiatives and campaigns encouraging individuals to perform random acts of kindness and spread positivity in their communities.

This powerful ripple effect all started with one person simply paying for someone else's coffee.

As you begin to share your gifts with the world, you are just one person, but you can't fathom the extent to which you will positively impact other people. When you immerse yourself in the process and truly commit to change, magic will happen. The ripple effect starts to spread all throughout your life and the lives of others, just like rings on the surface of a still pond, each one representing a beautiful season of possibility and change.

Chapter 19 Reflection

Let's start by imagining what your life looks like one year from now. No matter where you are on your Empty Nesting journey, just focus on the next upcoming year. Let's also assume that you consistently worked on your One Thing over this past year.

How did this impact your life overall? What kind of ripple effect did it have in multiple areas of your life? Did working on your One Thing lead you to work on other passion projects as well? When you feel better and have more confidence, that's often when you take more action on things you love to do. All the barriers just seem to be removed.

Write the date down in your journal one year from today. Here's an opening sentence you could use to get the ball rolling: For the past year, I have worked on _____, and I cannot believe how much my life has changed!

Then answer these questions:

 How are you showing up now that you have consistently worked on your One Thing? Like really knocked it out of the park?

 Describe your ideal day. How has that improved?

Are you happier and braver? Less scattered and stressed?

 Do you wake up more excited than you used to be?

 Are you lit up from within?

 Are you attracting new people, places, experiences, and things into your life?

 What are you no longer doing or accepting?

 Describe in detail how this has impacted your life and those around you.

 Did you decide to work on other passion projects as well with newfound confidence and energy?

 What was your favorite part about this past year?

 What are you most proud of?

Why one year? Because we overestimate what we can do in a day, but we underestimate what we can accomplish in a year by applying small, consistent effort to our goals.

As you immerse yourself in this exercise, remember that the future version of you is not a distant entity but rather an intrinsic part of you waiting to be unleashed. She's always been in there, but now we're shining a bright light on her and bringing those gifts to the surface. Defining and embodying the qualities of your envisioned self will ignite a powerful force that propels you toward your desired future. Embrace this vision, nurture it, and let it guide you as you continue on this transformative journey of self-discovery and growth.

Future you is a rock star.

Celebrate and Serve
The Joy of Giving Back

True celebration and service go hand in hand, for in uplifting others, we find the greatest joy and purpose within ourselves.

—OPRAH WINFREY

C elebrating personal achievements and milestones after undergoing a transformative journey like this is important. It symbolizes the culmination of your hard work, dedication, courage, and self-discovery. By designing your game plan for success, committing to your One Thing, and staying consistent, you have showcased your resilience and determination. Additionally, you honored the journey of self-reinvention and discovery.

Bravo!

Celebrating serves as a powerful reminder of the progress you have made, the obstacles you have overcome, and the strength you've gained. Redefining yourself took grit! Acknowledge the courage it took to embrace change, the vision it required to design a fulfilling new chapter of your life, and the commitment it demanded to become the best version of you. In essence, celebrating serves as a tribute to your unwavering spirit, resilience, and dedication to creating a life that embodies your true essence and passion in the Empty Nest.

I hope by now you have a completely different view of Empty Nesting—one that leaves you more inspired, prepared, and excited than before. You've discovered a lot about yourself, done a lot of internal and external work, and now it's time to celebrate! You've been on a profound journey of discovering your unique passions, finding new communities you align with, and preparing to embrace the joys of Empty Nesting.

Take time to celebrate all your accomplishments. Go out to dinner and share your wins with your family. Treat yourself to something special. Call an old friend and support each other's "glow-ups." My goal is to demystify the notion that when women share their wins, it seems like bragging. It's not. We all need support and encouragement. That's why I am currently planning a girls' night out called "Bubbles and Brags." I believe that by coming

Take time to celebrate all your accomplishments.

together, we can collectively affirm that sharing our wins is not selfish, but rather a celebration of everyone's achievements. It's a way to uplift and inspire each other to keep going, and a time to enjoy some good ol' champagne with our favorite friends.

Another way you could celebrate your accomplishments is by serving those in your community. It's a known fact your soul often finds its greatest joy in serving others. With children no longer requiring your constant attention, you will find yourself with newfound energy and additional time. This surplus of energy can be redirected toward serving local charities and making a positive impact. Empty Nesting is an ideal time to channel your passion and skills into endeavors that not only align with your values but benefit your community. Utilizing your talents to support local, national, and worldwide causes is fulfilling and so needed. Whether it's volunteering, mentoring, or sharing your expertise, your services become a meaningful way to give back and make a difference. It's also another great way to meet new people that share your new interests.

One local organization our family loves to support is Little Miracles.[64] Their mission is to help improve the lives of single mothers that have gone through tragic times. Since 2014, they have helped 150 families and contributed nearly 30,000 hours of service work. The process goes like this: A family gets nominated, then the team interviews the family and figures out how they can best serve them. One of my favorite projects we worked on was for the Jameson Family.

> *Empty nesting is an ideal time to channel your passion and skills into endeavors that not only align with your values but benefit your community.*

Mr. and Mrs. Jameson had adopted six special-needs teens, and Little Miracles wanted to treat them to a mini extreme home makeover. Over two days, one hundred people worked nonstop on their assigned projects. We renovated the kitchen, brought in new furniture, created a fun movie theater room, updated the backyard, decorated each bedroom with the teens' favorite Disney or Marvel movie murals, and had so much fun in the process. When the big reveal happened, the teens all jumped for joy and cried happy tears when they saw their new bedrooms.

It was priceless! Over the past ten years, I have worked on dozens of Little Miracles projects, and met incredible friends I have so much in common with. I plan to work with them during my Empty Nest years.

Research shows that engaging in acts of service not only benefits others but also enhances your own well-being. Studies have indicated that individuals who volunteer and give back to their communities experience increased levels of happiness, satisfaction, and better health. Joining hands with your community can create a ripple effect of kindness, compassion, and positivity, enriching your life and the lives of those around you. Embrace this with an open heart, and commit to spreading some joy through service. When we give of ourselves, we receive so much more in return. What a great way to celebrate!

Chapter 20 Reflection Exercise

For this exercise, I would like you to reflect on what celebration and service mean to you. Answer these questions in your journal.

CELEBRATION:

How do you best like to celebrate your achievements, big or small?

How can you commit to celebrating yourself, even if you haven't in the past?

In what ways can you mark this significant milestone in your life and honor your journey and growth?

Reflect on the past accomplishments that you celebrated. How did that celebration make you feel, and how can you replicate or enhance that feeling for your current achievements?

How can celebrating contribute to your overall well-being and motivate you to pursue future goals?

It's no small feat you made it through all the exercises in this book, so plan yourself a great celebration!

SERVICE:

When you think about service, answer these questions:

What causes or organizations deeply resonate with you and align with your values that you can contribute to in your Empty Nest years?

How can you leverage your skills, resources, or time to create a significant impact in the organizations or causes you are passionate about?

Reflect on a time when you contributed to a cause or an organization. How did that experience enrich your life, and how can you continue to integrate service into your Empty Nest journey?

Who can you enroll to help you with this service? Is there a group of people you like volunteering with?

Celebration and service are so important as you begin to wrap up this experience. Take some time to go back and read through your Reflection Exercises, and take it all in. It's amazing what you have just accomplished, and I can't wait to see what the future holds for you. As you reflect on your journey and growth, remember that celebrating your achievements and serving others are vital components for a fulfilling, purposeful life. Embrace the lessons learned, the perspectives gained, and the impact made as you move forward with renewed clarity and intention. The possibilities for your Empty Nest are endless, and I'm excited to witness the incredible transformation and success that lie ahead for you.

A Final Letter to My Readers
I Believe in You

She remembered who she was and the game changed.

—LALAH DELIA

D ear friend,
    As we reach the final pages of *The Almost Empty Nester*, I want to take a minute and congratulate you. I don't have much to teach you in this final chapter. This chapter is here to help you sit with all you have learned, discovered, and accomplished. Nice job! If you've made it this far, you deserve a celebration because it shows that you truly do want to prepare for and create an incredible Empty Nest. Give yourself the time and space to reflect on what you've just gone through, appreciate what you've started to work on, and acknowledge that it's worth celebrating.

You've been on an incredible journey throughout these twenty-one chapters. You embarked on a transformative path, rediscovered who you are before your kids leave the nest, and designed a future of your dreams. I want you to be immensely proud of the progress you've made. You've invested valuable time and energy in looking back at your journey as a mother. You've taken the courageous step of analyzing your current passions and identifying new projects that resonate with your Empty Nest plans. And you've taken actionable steps toward building your next best chapter. This introspection and work are a testament of your commitment of personal growth and self-discovery.

My hope is that this book has served as a guiding light, a source of comfort, and a reminder that you are an incredible woman and mother. You are not alone on this Empty Nest journey. As you step into this new chapter of your life, carry with you the knowledge that you are capable, resilient, and deserving of happiness. Embrace the beauty of change as your children begin to leave the nest, and enjoy all the mini magical moments you can. Remember to look for the glimmers. Always.

I'm glad you found the time to define and nurture your own goals and dreams. Embrace this next chapter with open arms, knowing that the best is yet to come. You now know you have the power to redefine what it means to be an Almost Empty Nester, or a brand-new Empty Nester, and to inspire others with your grace, resilience, and unwavering spirit. This can be such an exciting time in life filled with so much change and incredible possibility.

I want to thank you for picking up this book and taking a chance on yourself. And for being a part of this amazing community of women who are here to uplift and inspire each other. It has been an honor to guide you through the pages of *The Almost Empty Nester*. I have no doubt that you possess the strength, determination, and resilience to create a fulfilling and joyful life beyond the nest.

Wishing you all the love and joy you could possibly imagine.

With heartfelt gratitude,

xoxo,

Karla

Let's continue the conversation over at
THEEMPTYNESTERCLUB.COM

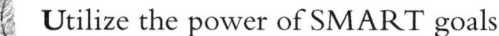
Chapter 21 Reflection Exercise

Let's take a moment to express gratitude to the present you for taking the first steps towards your future dreams. Embrace this opportunity and let the wisdom and guidance you've learned along the way inspire and uplift you as you move forward. Here's to your bright FUTURE:

 **F**ormulate your new game plan.

Utilize the power of SMART goals.

Take one step at a time.

Understand that success is about consistency, not perfection.

Roll with your One Thing, and watch all the ripples that come from it.

Embrace a new tribe, and find ways to serve your community.

For this last exercise, I invite you to write a heartfelt letter from your future self, with all that she has accomplished, to the mother you are today. Let this letter be a celebration of the progress you've made and a source of encouragement for the journey ahead. Express gratitude to the present you for taking the first steps toward your dreams. Embrace this opportunity, and let the wisdom and guidance of your future self inspire and uplift you.

Describe in detail every amazing new person, place, opportunity, or thing that has come into your life. Acknowledge the determination and resilience that brought you to where you are now. Embrace the excitement of the possibilities that lie before you.

And be sure to thank the current you for having the clarity and courage to begin.

You are an amazing gift to this world, and I am rooting for you!

xoxo,

Karla

The Gardener of Souls

In the garden of life, a mother sows,
Nurturing her children with love that flows,
Seeds of dreams, she carefully tends,
Watching her children bloom and ascend.
Proudly watch as they take to the skies
Spreading their wings while you dry your eyes.
You've loved and nurtured them so dearly.
You've done a great job. I mean this sincerely.
To the miracle mothers, the gardeners of souls,
Now that your nest is beginning to unfold,
It's time for you to blossom and bloom anew,
Rediscovering passion and dreams just for you.
There's joy to be found in this Empty Nest journey
It's important to start working on your future nest early.
Embrace this time and fall in love with your future.
The road will be less bumpy, and the ride much smoother.
Mothers deserve to feel fulfilled and bright,
Even as their children take off in flight.
It's time for women's gifts to be unfurled,
Together, we can illuminate and transform the world.
When women rise, we all climb higher
Awakening our souls to our internal fire
For in your heart, a universe resides,
Ready to bloom and conquer the tides.
So let your light shine, my dear miracle mother.
You're special indeed. You are like no other.
Gardeners of souls, with love's pure light,
I wish this next chapter to be one of the best in your life.

THANK YOUS AND ACKNOWLEDGMENTS

To say "it takes a village" might be an understatement regarding this project. Starting out as a brand-new author, I had an idea in my mind of what I *thought* it would take to write a book. Tack on an entire extra year of work, research, editing, rewriting, etc., I have learned so much from so many, and I'm grateful for your love, patience, and input. I want to take a minute to acknowledge and thank the many people who helped with this project.

To my mom, thank you so much for being the best mom anyone could ask for. You are a true example of what unconditional love feels like. Thank you for supporting me, believing in me, and always encouraging me. I love you with all my heart.

To my husband, Mark. Thank you for the past thirty incredible years. I love and appreciate you so much. Thank you for believing in my big ideas and for being my biggest champion. Simply put, "Life is better with you."

To my three daughters: Kenzie, Riley, and Katie. This book is my love letter to you. You've brought so much joy and laughter into my life, more than I could have ever imagined. I am forever grateful I get to be your mama. I can't wait to witness the positive impact you have on the world. I love you dearly.

To my friends and family, thank you for your love, support, and words of encouragement. It means the world to me, always has. I am so grateful for my village. Special thanks to Erin, Kate, and Terry for getting me started on this project and helping me take this across the finish line. Love you, Soul Sisters.

To my book cover concept designer, Michelle Rayner. Your artwork is stunning and exactly what I envisioned my cover to look like. You know I love feathers, sunrises, and everything they represent. You incorporated all of them beautifully. I'm so glad I got to work with you.

To Stacy Dymalski, thank you for teaching me how to be a better writer and storyteller. What I have learned from you is priceless.

To my brand and web designer Cristina Horvath. The way you "beautify" everything in the world is hard to describe. Thank you for knowing me so well and bringing to life my vision for theemptynesterclub.com. You are truly a gift to this world. Love you forever, C.

To my creative director, Hannah Musgrove, for all of your design input and development. Working with you has been a delight, and I can't wait to see what we create together in the future.

To Larissa Salazar and the entire Brand Builders family. I could not have done this without you. I hope every human who wants to write a book, become a speaker, or build a brand for their business finds you because the world deserves to work with people like you. Thank you for helping me get clear on my audience and how I could best serve them, believing in my vision, and for making me a better person.

To the entire StoryBuilders team, especially Sarah, the ultimate whip-snapping project manager, and Tracy, the maker of all things beautiful. You have been my North Star throughout the entire publishing process. And a special thanks to my cover designer, Rochelle, interior designer, Najdan, my publishing team, Nichole, Josiah, and Bill. Every single member of the StoryBuilders team is authentic, service-oriented, and top-notch at what you do. Partnering with you is an honor and a gift. I can't wait to get working with you on the next book. Everything you do is a chef's kiss!

And especially to all the mothers who read this book and worked through the exercises, you are my heroes. My wish for you is that you create the best Empty Nest you can imagine. Now go share your gifts with the world!

P.S. If you would like to personally reach out to and work with any of the companies/partners I have listed here, please do so. They are incredible, and most of them offer discounts when you say you were referred by The Empty Nester Club. You can find their links on our TENC Partner page.

DO IT FOR THE LOVE

When considering which organizations I wanted The Empty Nester Club to support, I focused on aligning with passion and purpose-driven charities. Do It For the Love® combines two true loves in my life: music and helping others. Founded by Michael and Sara Franti, Do It For the Love® is an organization that provides hope, healing, and music to thousands of people.[65] Year 2023 marked their tenth anniversary. To date, they have reached over twelve thousand people, granted over three thousand wishes, and produced over five hundred thousand minutes of music that have been enjoyed. From the likes of Luke Combs and Billie Eilish, Do It For the Love® has impacted the lives of many. By providing a much-needed break from the routine of doctors and medication, Wish recipients come away from their experience with a strong sense of hope for the future. Having survived breast cancer twice myself, I deeply understand on a soul level how much music can positively impact your outlook on your prognosis. During my countless MRIs and CT scans, Michael's music helped me tremendously through my treatments. I'm proud to be a part of the Soulrockerfam.

For more information on how you can get involved with this incredible organization, go to doitforthelove.org.

ShelterBox

You see it on the news: mothers, fathers, daughters, and sons, left homeless after disasters like an earthquake or typhoon, or after a conflict. The U.N. estimates there are 120 million of these forcibly displaced people around the world as I type. There are currently more refugees now than ever before.

So, who cares, and does anything about it? ShelterBox USA! The disaster relief agency is rated 100 percent on charity navigator for its ability to get a durable tent, water purification kit, solar lantern, cookware set, and more life saving supplies to the most vulnerable people.

A seamstress in a tsunami-ravaged village in Indonesia got back on her feet, sewing again under the porch of her sturdy ShelterBox tent. A father in Syria, rocked by an earthquake and an endless war, beamed when he got his ShelterBox kit, including thermal onesies for his infants. In Ukraine, a resident used a repair kit to shore up the missing wall of her house and did her work using solar light. Since its beginning, ShelterBox has delivered aid to over two million people in almost 100 countries, and turned despair into stability, angst into a future.

ShelterBox gets into almost impossible to reach places with help of its extensive network of partners with tireless dedication, creativity, and without having any political affiliations.

There's a photo of ShelterBox USA president Kerri Murray that tells an amazing story. You see Kerri, a Western woman in a polo shirt and jeans, delivering a highly coveted cookware kit to a woman in the Atlas Mountains of Morocco. The woman is wearing all-white, symbolic of being a widow. Her husband died in the devastating September 2023 earthquake. The Moroccan widow, being handed a white box of stainless-steel pots pans and more in a remote, flattened village, is smiling. She can now more easily cook a meal for friends and family.

I can't travel to Morocco to help widows, or get tents into Gaza to shelter children, or put up a mosquito net in Grenada, where islanders are petrified of getting a mosquito-borne illness like dengue fever after hurricane Beryl.

But ShelterBox will get the critical supplies there. Help me help ShelterBox continue their important work.

WWW.SHELTERBOXUSA.ORG/HOME-PAGE/MEDIA/

REFERENCES

1. Shelton, Ron, dir. 1996. *Tin Cup*. Regency Enterprises.
2. Daraman, I. (2022, April 4). *Empty nest divorce statistics*. Tips For Efficiency. https://tipsforefficiency.com/empty-nest-divorce-statistics/
3. Williamson, Marianne. 1996. *A Return to Love: Reflections on the Principles of A Course in Miracles*. New York: HarperCollins.
4. Yuvashree Murugan, Padmavathi Nagarajan, DKS Subrahmanyam, Shivanand Kattimani, Severity of loneliness, depression and perceived social support in adults in the empty nest stage of the family life cycle and the influence of using digital technology, Asian Journal of Psychiatry, Volume 76, 2022, 103245, ISSN 1876-2018, https://doi.org/10.1016/j.ajp.2022.103245. https://www.sciencedirect.com/science/article/pii/S187620182200243X
5. Ibid.
6. Victoria Department of Health. 2012. "Empty nest syndrome." Better Health Channel. https://www.betterhealth.vic.gov.au/health/healthyliving/empty-nest-syndrome.
7. U.S. Department of Health and Human Services. 2023. "New Surgeon General Advisory Raises Alarm about the Devastating Impact of the Epidemic of Loneliness and Isolation in the United States." HHS.gov. https://www.hhs.gov/about/news/2023/05/03/new-surgeon-general-advisory-raises-alarm-about-devastating-impact-epidemic-loneliness-isolation-united-states.html.
8. Oxford University Press. n.d. "Empty Nest Syndrome." Oxford Languages. Accessed July 25, 2024. https://languages.oup.com/google-dictionary-en/.

9. Lawrenz, Lori. 2021. "What Now? Understanding Empty Nest Syndrome." Psych Central. https://psychcentral.com/health/empty-nest-syndrome#empty-nest-defined.

10. Ibid.

11. Ibid.

12. Ibid.

13. Ibid.

14. Chapman, Gary. 2000. *The Five Love Languages: How to Express Heartfelt Commitment to Your Mate.* Chicago: Strand Publishing.

15. Angelou, Maya. n.d. "Quotable Quote." Goodreads. Accessed July 25, 2024. https://www.goodreads.com/quotes/7273813-do-the-best-you-can-until-you-know-better-then.

16. Styles, Harry. n.d. "Quotable Quotes." Goodreads. Accessed July 25, 2024. https://www.goodreads.com/quotes/11563572-fill-up-your-own-cup-and-let-them-fall-in.

17. Dr. Seuss. n.d. "Quotable Quote." Goodreads. Accessed July 25, 2024. https://www.goodreads.com/quotes/187115-why-fit-in-when-you-were-born-to-stand-out.

18. Duhigg, Charles. 2012. *The Power of Habit: Why We Do What We Do in Life and Business.* New York: Random House Publishing Group.

19. Roosevelt, Theodore. 2011. "It Is Not the Critic Who Counts." Theodore Roosevelt Conservation Partnership. https://www.trcp.org/2011/01/18/it-is-not-the-critic-who-counts/.

20. Ware, Bronnie. 2012. *The Top Five Regrets of the Dying: A Life Transformed by the Dearly Departing.* Carlsbad, CA: Hay House.

21. Sidford, Terry. 2023. *Truth. Courage. Love.* Park City, UT: Surrogate Press.

22. Hendricks, Gay. 2021. *The Genius Zone: The Breakthrough Process to End Negative Thinking and Live in True Creativity.* New York: St. Martin's Publishing Group.

23. Sidford, Terry. 2023. *Truth. Courage. Love.* Park City, UT: Surrogate Press.

24. Brown, Brené. 2020. *The Gifts of Imperfection.* Center City, Minnesota: Hazelden Publishing.

25. Keng, S. L., M. J. Smoski, and C. J. Robins. 2011. "Effects of mindfulness on psychological health: a review of empirical studies." Clinical psychology review 31 (6): 1041–1056.

26. TODAY. 2023. "Julia Roberts, Mahershala Ali talk new Netflix thriller, parenting." YouTube. https://www.youtube. com/watch?v=XiQ8KUd56Us.

27. Wolf, Kelley. 2022. *FLOW Finding Love Over Worry: A Recipe for Living Joyfully.* N.p.: Three Trees.

28. Wolf, Kelley. n.d. "About Kelley." FLOW by Kelley Wolf. Accessed July 25, 2024. https://flowbykelleywolf.com/ about-kelley-2/.

29. Vilhauer, J. (n.d.). *How your thinking affects your brain chemistry.* Psychology Today. https://www.psychologytoday.com/us/ blog/living-forward/202304/how-your-thinking-affects-your-brain-chemistry

30. Dispenza, Joe. 2013. *Breaking The Habit of Being Yourself: How to Lose Your Mind and Create a New One.* Carlsbad, CA: Hay House.

31. Ibid.

32. Ibid.

33. Nevelle, Dirk. 2023. "Rediscover Your Passion and Purpose in Life Before Your Kids Leave the Nest." YouTube. https:// www.youtube.com/watch?v=FhtWEc7XE1I.

34. Kaku, Michio. 2024. "Albert Einstein - Physics, Relativity, Nobel Prize." Britannica. https://www.britannica.com/ biography/Albert-Einstein/From-graduation-to-the-miracle-year-of-scientific-theories.

35. Wall, Daniel. 2023. "So I Interviewed The Biggest Songwriter in The World..." YouTube. https://www.youtube.com/watch?v=85aTwqNZIpE.

36. Merriam-Webster. 2024. "Decide Definition & Meaning." Merriam-Webster. https://www.merriam-webster.com/dictionary/decide.

37. Hernandez, Morela. 2018. "The Impossibility of Focusing on Two Things at Once." MIT Sloan Management Review. https://sloanreview.mit.edu/article/the-impossibility-of-focusing-on-two-things-at-once/.

38. Cherry, Kendra. 2023. "Multitasking, Productivity, and Brain Health." Verywell Mind. https://www.verywellmind.com/multitasking-2795003.

39. Le Cunff, Anne-Laure. n.d. "Cognitive bottlenecks: the inherent limits of the thinking mind." Ness Labs. Accessed July 25, 2024. https://nesslabs.com/cognitive-bottlenecks.

40. Indiana University. n.d. "Viola Davis: University Honors and Awards: Indiana University." University Honors & Awards. Accessed July 25, 2024. https://honorsandawards.iu.edu/awards/honoree/9349.html.

41. Rosenbloom, Michael H., Jeremy D. Schmahmann, and Bruce H. Price. 2012. "The functional neuroanatomy of decision-making." *The Journal of neuropsychiatry and clinical neurosciences* 24 (3): 266-77.

42. Andersone, Nelda. 2023. "Decoding the Inner Critic's Origins and Purpose." Psychology Today. https://www.psychologytoday.com/us/blog/human-inner-dynamics/202312/decoding-the-inner-critics-origins-and-purpose.

43. Ibid.

44. Stefon, Matt. 2024. "Sara Blakely | Biography, Spanx, & Facts." Britannica. https://www.britannica.com/money/Sara-Blakely.

45. Virtues For Life. n.d. "Native American Tale Two Wolves." Virtues For Life: The heart of everyday living. Accessed July 25, 2024. https://www.virtuesforlife.com/two-wolves/.

46. Cherry, Kendra. 2023. "Negative Bias: Why We're Hardwired for Negativity." Verywell Mind. https://www.verywellmind.com/negative-bias-4589618.

47. Rushdie, Salman. 2024. "J.K. Rowling | Biography, Full Name, Books, & Facts." Britannica. https://www.britannica.com/biography/J-K-Rowling.

48. Bentzen-Mercer, Cynthia, and Kimberly K. Rath. 2024. *Now, Near, Next: A Practical Guide for Mid-Career Women to Move from Professional Serendipity to Intentional Advancement.* Herndon, VA: Amplify Publishing.

49. Ibid.

50. Ibid.

51. Damaschino, Anthony. 2023. *The Empty Nest Blueprint: Plan, Pursue, and Thrive for the Most Underrated Stage of Your Life.* Danville, CA: Infinite Space Publishing.

52. Encyclopaedia Britannica. 2024. "Vera Wang | Biography, Wedding Dresses, Fashion, & Brand." Britannica. https://www.britannica.com/biography/Vera-Wang.

53. Haughey, Duncan. 2014. "A Brief History of SMART Goals." Project Smart. https://www.projectsmart.co.uk/smart-goals/brief-history-of-smart-goals.php.

54. @growordie_. n.d. "Growordie." TikTok. Accessed July 25, 2024. https://www.tiktok.com/@growordie_.

55. Hardy, Darren. 2010. *The Compound Effect.* New York: Vanguard Press.

56. Clear, James. 2018. *Atomic Habits: An Easy and Proven Way to Build Good Habits and Break Bad Ones.* New York: Penguin Random House.

57. Ibid.

58. Hendricks, Gay. 2010. *The Big Leap: Conquer Your Hidden Fear and Take Life to the Next Level.* New York: HarperCollins.

59. Skolnicki, Cherylanne. n.d. "Revive." Brilliant Balance. Accessed July 25, 2024. https://brilliant-balance.com/revive.

60. Hanke, Stacey. 2018. "Three Steps To Overcoming Resistance." Forbes. https://www.forbes.com/sites/forbescoachescouncil/2018/08/14/three-steps-to-overcoming-resistance/.

61. Kyprianides, A., M.J. Easterbrook, and R. Brown. 2019. "Group identities benefit well-being by satisfying needs." *Journal of Experimental Social Psychology* 84.

62. ShelterBox. n.d. "ShelterBox History." ShelterBox USA. Accessed July 25, 2024. https://www.shelterboxusa.org/history/.

63. Firozi, Paulina. 2014. "378 people 'pay it forward' at Starbucks." USA Today. https://www.usatoday.com/story/news/nation-now/2014/08/21/378-people-pay-it-forward-at-fla-starbucks/14380109/.

64. Little Miracles. n.d. Little Miracles Utah: Serve. Connect. Inspire. Accessed July 25, 2024. https://www.littlemiraclesutah.org/.

65. Do It For The Love. n.d. "Our Story." Do It For The Love. Accessed July 25, 2024. https://www.doitforthelove.org/.

For more info on the author and upcoming projects, go to
THEEMPTYNESTERCLUB.COM

www.ingramcontent.com/pod-product-compliance
Lightning Source LLC
Chambersburg PA
CBHW070918120626
46546CB00001B/316